"Any Christian perplexed by t ... eternal and temporal kingdom. ... indispensable guide in sorting out the confused thinking that entangles the church today. This succinct and timely alternative to neo-Calvinism's transformationist vision lays the groundwork for a wide-ranging and urgently needed discussion about two-kingdom theology's implications for education, the workplace, and politics."

Richard M. Gamble, Anna Margaret Ross Alexander Professor of History and Political Science, Hillsdale College

"For some years now, I've been asking students to read works by Prof. David VanDrunen of Westminster Seminary California. VanDrunen has a gift for recovering themes from the political theology of the Reformation and demonstrating their continuing relevance. In this book, VanDrunen shows that the Reformation's two-kingdoms theology allows Christians to faithfully navigate a course between, on the one hand, investing excessive hope in earthly government or, on the other, retreating from political life into isolationist enclaves. Particularly welcome is his emphasis on the liberty of biblical Christians to reach differing conclusions about how our political engagement might glorify God."

Randy Beck, Professor of Law, University of Georgia School of Law

"For those interested in a Reformed two-kingdom model, I can think of no better book to start than *Living in God's Two Kingdoms*. Redemptive-historical in scope, heavenly minded in emphasis, and gentle in tone, David VanDrunen has made a great contribution to the ongoing discussion of the relationship of Christianity and culture."

Danny E. Olinger, General Secretary, Committee on Christian Education of the Orthodox Presbyterian Church

"Evangelicals today, including those within the Reformed community, have become annoyed by the competing (and, in a few cases, embarrassingly inadequate) "transformationalist" programs offered by leading Christian thinkers. With clarity and concision, David VanDrunen has offered an alternative perspective that liberates the Christian conscience to sincerely engage society without relegating the sovereignty of God over "every square inch" of it. *Living in God's Two Kingdoms* will certainly stimulate debate and force Christians to reevaluate the relationship between Christ and culture."

Ryan McIlhenny, Assistant Professor of Humanities, Providence Christian College

LIVING
IN
GOD'S
TWO
KINGDOMS

LIVING
IN
GOD'S
TWO
KINGDOMS

A Biblical Vision *for* Christianity *and* Culture

David VanDrunen

CROSSWAY®

WHEATON, ILLINOIS

Interior design and typesetting: Lakeside Design Plus
Cover design: Dual Identity
First printing 2010
Printed in the United States of America

Scripture quotations are from the ESV® Bible (The Holy Bible, English Standard Version®), copyright © 2001 by Crossway, a publishing ministry of Good News Publishers. Used by permission. All rights reserved.

All emphases in Scripture quotations have been added.

Trade Paperback ISBN: 978-1-4335-1404-3
PDF ISBN: 978-1-4335-1405-0
Mobipocket ISBN: 978-1-4335-1406-7
ePub ISBN: 978-1-4335-2452-3

Library of Congress Cataloging-in-Publication Data
VanDrunen, David, 1971–
    Living in God's two kingdoms : a biblical vision for Christianity and culture / David VanDrunen.
        p. cm.
    Includes bibliographical references and index.
        ISBN 978-1-4335-1404-3 (tpb)—ISBN 978-1-4335-1405-0 (pdf)—
    ISBN 978-1-4335-1406-7 (mobipocket)— ISBN 978-1-4335-2452-3 (ePub)
        1. Christianity and culture. 2. Reformed Church—Doctrines. 3. Two kingdoms (Lutheran theology) I. Title.
    BR115.C8V295   2010
    261—dc22

Crossway is a publishing ministry of Good News Publishers.
5LP   28   27   26   25   24   23   22   21   20   19   18

Contents

Acknowledgments

I WISH TO EXPRESS my sincere thanks to many people for the counsel, feedback, and encouragement they have offered to me in the course of planning and producing this book. First, I am grateful to the staff at Crossway for providing another excellent experience in bringing a book into existence. Allan Fisher and Tara Davis deserve special thanks, the first for his initial interest in this project and the latter for her very helpful editorial work.

My sabbatical during the spring semester of 2009 provided the ideal opportunity to write a number of chapters in this book. My thanks go to the faculty and board of Westminster Seminary California for granting me this study leave. Special thanks to others who helped to make it possible, especially the students who put up with an intensive form of my Christian Life course in January 2009 and to Kim Riddlebarger, who taught another course that spring in my absence. This is also my first—but certainly not last—opportunity to express in print my gratitude to the Center for the Study of Law and Religion at Emory University, and especially to John Witte and Amy Wheeler, for their warm hospitality in hosting me during my sabbatical.

I also thank the many people who were generous enough to read all or sections of the book and to offer me their comments of various kinds: Steve Baugh, Randy Beck, John Earnest, Bryan Estelle, John Fesko, Jim Gidley, Bob Godfrey, Dennis Johnson, Zach Keele,

Ryan McIhlenny, Danny Olinger, Ron Prins, Bob Strimple, Matt Tuininga, and Tom VanDrunen. The encouragement was appreciated; the advice was always weighed and often heeded.

To Katherine and Jack: thank you again for everything.

Finally, thanks to the Lunchbox for twisting my arm one pleasant, southern California autumn evening and telling me that it was time to write this book. Maybe you were right, maybe you were wrong, but the work has been its own reward. Here's to many enjoyable conversations over the years about the two kingdoms and matters germane—whether in Dubuque, Escondido, Evanston, Galena, Green Lake, Hull, Iowa City, Las Vegas, Minneapolis, Northfield, Outing, Waterloo, or Wilmette. May there be many more.

Introduction

Christianity, Culture, and the Two Kingdoms

IN PERHAPS THE MOST FAMOUS BOOK ever written on the topic of Christianity and culture, H. Richard Niebuhr stated: "It is helpful to remember that the question of Christianity and civilization is by no means a new one; that Christian perplexity in this area has been perennial, and that the problem has been an enduring one through all the Christian centuries."[1] You have begun reading another in a long line of books that deal with this perplexing and perennial topic. I have written such a volume for two primary reasons.

First, the issue of Christianity and culture is one of immense importance and relevance. If you are a serious Christian, you probably think about the Christianity and culture question on a regular basis, whether you realize it or not. Every time you reflect upon what your faith has to do with your job, your schoolwork, your political views, the books you read, or the movies you see, you confront the problem of Christianity and culture. When you consider what

---

[1]H. Richard Niebuhr, *Christ and Culture* (New York: Harper, 1951), 2.

responsibilities your church might have with respect to contemporary political controversies or economic development, you again come face-to-face with the Christianity and culture issue. It is no accident that so many of the greatest minds in the history of the Christian church have wrestled with this problem and that so many books have been written about it. Just think how much time, energy, and passion topics like religion and modern science or faith and politics generate in the Christian community. Even so, this subject is about much more than simply these overtly "cultural" topics. Developing a coherent view of Christianity and culture demands wrestling with some of the most fundamental truths of the Christian faith. A faithful biblical theology of Christianity and culture depends upon a proper view of creation, providence, the image of God, sin, the work of Christ, salvation, the church, and eschatology. Therefore I write this book to address not a narrow issue but one that confronts us with the fundamentals of Christian faith and life. This project thus has a very personal dimension for me—it has been an exercise in expressing and defending many things that are most precious to me as a believer in Christ.

Second, I write this book out of a growing conviction that contemporary conversations about Christianity and culture are on the wrong track and that the perspective presented in these pages, largely overlooked today, offers a biblical corrective that can help to get discussion back on the right track. Though a multitude of voices are contributing to the contemporary conversations, many of them have a great deal in common. Some of the themes frequently emphasized in contemporary conversations are right on target and very important for a sound view of Christianity and culture. Other themes, I fear, present a distorted view of Christian cultural engagement and its relationship to the church and to the hope of the new heaven and new earth.

Let me mention a few things that the contemporary voices get right. First, many contemporary voices emphasize that God is the Creator of all things, including material and physical things. God is king of all areas of life, and human beings are accountable to him in everything they do. Many contemporary voices also helpfully remind us that it is good for Christians to be involved in a variety of cultural pursuits. Christians should not withdraw from the broader culture but should take up cultural tasks with joy and express their Christian faith through them. Every lawful occupation is honorable. These voices also remind us that the effects of sin penetrate all aspects of life. Christians must therefore be vigilant in their cultural pursuits, perceiving and rejecting the sinful patterns in cultural life and striving after obedience to God's will in everything. Finally, many contemporary voices stress that the true Christian hope is not for a disembodied life as a soul in heaven but for the resurrection and new heaven and new earth. All of these affirmations are true and helpful. ✓

Unfortunately, other themes popular in the contemporary conversations are problematic. For example, many contemporary voices assert that God is *redeeming* all legitimate cultural activities and institutions and that Christians are therefore called to transform them accordingly and to build the kingdom of God through this work.[2] Some advocates of this position claim that redemption is God's work of *restoration*, empowering human beings to pick up again the task of the first human beings, Adam and Eve, and to develop human culture as they were originally called to do. This redemptive transformation of present human culture begins a process that will culminate in the new creation—the new heaven and new earth. According to this vision of Christian cultural engagement, our cultural products will adorn the eternal city.

Many talented authors present such ideas as an exciting and inspiring vision, but are they biblically sound? I believe that they are *not* true to Scripture, and therefore I offer a biblical alternative in this book. I refer to this alternative as a "two-kingdoms" doctrine. Though many writers in recent years have ignored, mischaracterized, or slandered the idea of "two kingdoms," it has a venerable place in the annals of Christian theology. It stands in the line of

---

[2]The terms "transform" and "transformation" have various connotations. I believe that Christians should transform culture in the sense that they seek to have a beneficial influence on this world as they perform cultural activities with excellence and interpret them rightly. In this book I am critical of the idea of transforming culture, however, insofar as it implies that Christians are to "redeem" culture and that their godly cultural products will be incorporated into the new creation.

Christian thinking famously articulated by Augustine in *The City of God*, developed in the Lutheran and Calvinist Reformations, and brought to greater maturity in the post-Reformation Reformed tradition.[3] Many writers today seem to associate a two-kingdoms doctrine with unwarranted dualisms, secularism, moral neutrality in social life, or even the denial of Christ's universal kingship. Perhaps some versions of the two-kingdoms doctrine have fit such stereotypes. My task in this book is not to defend everything that has ever gone by the name "two kingdoms," but to expound a two-kingdoms approach that is thoroughly grounded in the story of Scripture and biblical doctrine. It embraces the heritage of Augustine and the Reformation and seeks to develop and strengthen it further. I will strive to present it in an accessible and useful form to the church in the early twenty-first century.

This two-kingdoms doctrine strongly affirms that God has made all things, that sin corrupts all aspects of life, that Christians should be active in human culture, that all lawful cultural vocations are honorable, that all people are accountable to God in every activity, and that Christians should seek to live out the implications

---

[3] For a detailed argument in support of this historical claim, see David VanDrunen, *Natural Law and the Two Kingdoms: A Study in the Development of Reformed Social Thought* (Grand Rapids: Eerdmans, 2010), chaps. 2–6. To clarify one matter for readers who may be interested, I do not believe that Augustine's "two cities" refers to the same thing as the "two kingdoms" that I discuss in this book. Both are biblical concepts and both should be affirmed, but they do not describe identical realities. In short, Augustine, in *The City of God*, described two cities, one consisting of true believers and destined for eternal blessing, and the other consisting of unbelievers and destined for eternal condemnation. Each person is a citizen of one city, and one city only, though the two cities necessarily intermingle in this present world. The Reformed tradition, from which I write, has understood *both* of the two kingdoms as *God's*. God rules all things, but rules the affairs of this world in two fundamentally different ways. Christians are therefore citizens of two "kingdoms" but one "city." Another important biblical distinction is between "two ages"—this age and the age to come—which is a significant theme in Paul's epistles. I believe that the Pauline distinction between the two ages is also different from the two-kingdoms distinction, though they are compatible since they are both true. Whereas the two-kingdoms doctrine primarily explains the twofold way in which God governs this present world, the two-ages doctrine primarily concerns an eschatological distinction and tension between this world and the next. And whereas both of the two kingdoms are legitimate and divinely-ordained (though corrupted by sin in this world), Paul's presentation of "this age" focuses upon its evil and demonic character and its rebellion against God (e.g., see 2 Cor. 4:4; Gal. 1:4; Eph. 2:2). Thus in Romans 12:2 (when he is thinking in terms of the two ages) Paul exhorts Christians not to be conformed to this age, while in Romans 13:1–7 (when he is thinking in terms of the two kingdoms) he exhorts them to be submissive to civil authorities as divinely-established officers of God.

of their faith in their daily vocations. A Christian, however, does *not* have to adopt a redemptive vision of culture in order to affirm these important truths. A biblical two-kingdoms doctrine provides another compelling way to do so. According to this doctrine, God is *not redeeming* the cultural activities and institutions of this world, but is *preserving* them through the covenant he made with all living creatures through Noah in Genesis 8:20–9:17. God himself rules this "common kingdom," and thus it is not, as some writers describe it, the "kingdom of man." This kingdom is in no sense a realm of moral neutrality or autonomy. God makes its institutions and activities honorable, though only for temporary and provisional purposes. Simultaneously, God *is redeeming* a people for himself, by virtue of the covenant made with Abraham and brought to glorious fulfillment in the work of the Lord Jesus Christ, who has completed Adam's original task once and for all. These redeemed people are citizens of the "redemptive kingdom," whom God is gathering now in the church and will welcome into the new heaven and new earth at Christ's glorious return. Until that day, Christians live as members of both kingdoms, discharging their proper duties in each. They rejoice to be citizens of heaven through membership in the church, but also recognize that for the time being they are *living in Babylon*, striving for justice and excellence in their cultural labors, out of love for Christ and their neighbor, as sojourners and exiles in a land that is not their lasting home.[4]

In order to introduce and explain this two-kingdoms vision more clearly, I now briefly describe some of the prominent voices in contemporary conversations about Christianity and culture. All of these voices, in various ways, defend a redemptive model of Christian cultural engagement. After I describe their views, I will turn readers' attention back to the two-kingdoms alternative and summarize the biblical defense of the two-kingdoms doctrine that will unfold in the chapters to come.

---

[4]I develop the "Babylon" theme in part 2. For other recent attempts to examine the Christianity and culture question in part through the biblical motif of "Babylon," see Richard John Neuhaus, *American Babylon: Notes of a Christian Exile* (New York: Basic, 2009) and Jason J. Stellman, *Dual Citizens: Worship and Life between the Already and the Not Yet* (Orlando: Reformation Trust, 2009). Augustine long ago utilized the Babylon theme; e.g., see *City of God*, 19.26.

Contemporary Voices: The Redemptive Transformation of Culture

In the contemporary conversations about Christianity and culture, there is perhaps no voice more eloquent than what is sometimes referred to as "neo-Calvinism." This school of thought traces back most immediately to the work of Dutch philosopher and jurist Herman Dooyeweerd (1894–1977), and it also *claims* to be heir of the Dutch theologian and statesman Abraham Kuyper (1837–1920) and of the Reformer John Calvin (1509–1564).[5] "Neo-Calvinism" has been influential not only in many Reformed and evangelical churches but has provided inspiration for many Christian schools and colleges in recent generations. My own early education, in both church and school, was significantly shaped by this line of thought. A number of friends, pastors, and theologians that I respect embrace its views. It gets many things correct and presents an attractive vision for Christianity and culture in many respects. It helpfully combats forms of Christianity that are indifferent to mundane cultural activity or see the faith as only relevant on Sundays. In the end, however, it misreads some important biblical themes and offers a distorted theology of Christian cultural engagement.

One fascinating thing about the current scene is that many other prominent Christian voices sound so similar to neo-Calvinism. When neo-Calvinists speak about Platonic and dualistic tendencies in the contemporary church, the redemptive transformation of culture, and the connection of cultural work to the kingdom of God and the new creation, they have a lot of company. I could cite many examples, but I focus on two that have gained considerable attention in the Christian world in recent years: the New Perspective on Paul (as exemplified by N. T. Wright) and the emerging (or emergent) church (as exemplified by Brian McLaren). Though advocates of neo-Calvinism, the New Perspective on Paul, and the emerging church certainly do not hold identical views on all issues, they show

---

[5]See VanDrunen, *Natural Law and the Two Kingdoms*, chaps. 7 and 9. In these chapters I discuss neo-Calvinism in more scholarly detail than I can treat it here.

mutual respect for each other's work[6] and, most significantly, they share a common vision that the redemptive transformation of culture is central to the Christian life.

Contemporary Neo-Calvinism

Neo-Calvinism is a diverse movement in certain respects, but its proponents are united by many common themes. Two contemporary advocates of the neo-Calvinist vision have summarized "neo-Calvinism" in three points: first, grace restores nature through redemption in Christ; second, God is sovereign and orders all of reality; and third, the original cultural mandate of Genesis 1 has ongoing relevance.[7] This is a concise and accurate summary, but it may be helpful to unpack the tenets of neo-Calvinism at a little more length. To do so, I refer especially to two books that present a neo-Calvinist perspective: Albert Wolters's *Creation Regained* and Cornelius Plantinga's *Engaging God's World*.[8] These writers do not necessarily agree with each other on every specific issue, but their general vision of Christianity and culture is the same. Their books are accessible and winsomely written, and they have been influential in many Christian schools and colleges.

Perhaps the most important thing to know initially about neo-Calvinism is that it presents the story of Scripture as the story of *creation, fall,* and *redemption*. Recognizing this pattern forms the heart of a Christian worldview, according to neo-Calvinism. What this means is that "all has been created good, including the full range of human cultures that emerge when humans act according

---

[6]Note, for example, the debt to Wright expressed in Brian D. McLaren, *Everything Must Change: Jesus, Global Crises, and a Revolution of Hope* (Nashville: Thomas Nelson, 2007), chap. 15. Several recent books by neo-Calvinist authors also express debt to Wright: e.g., Albert M. Wolters, *Creation Regained: Biblical Basics for a Reformational Worldview*, 2d ed. (Grand Rapids: Eerdmans, 2005), 127; Craig G. Bartholomew and Michael W. Goheen, *The Drama of Scripture: Finding Our Place in the Biblical Story* (Grand Rapids: Baker Academic, 2004), 13, 21, 197, 199; and Michael W. Goheen and Craig G. Bartholomew, *Living at the Crossroads: An Introduction to Christian Worldview* (Grand Rapids: Baker Academic, 2008), 4, 107, 144.

[7]Bartholomew and Goheen, *Living at the Crossroads*, 16.

[8]Subsequent citations from Wolters's book will come from the first edition: Albert M. Wolters, *Creation Regained: Biblical Basics for a Reformational Worldview* (Grand Rapids: Eerdmans, 1985). Cornelius Plantinga Jr., *Engaging God's World: A Christian Vision of Faith, Learning, and Living* (Grand Rapids: Eerdmans, 2002).

to God's design. But all has been corrupted by evil, including not only culture but also the natural world. So all—the whole cosmos—must be redeemed by Jesus Christ the Lord."[9] Wolters and Plantinga share a general conviction that God created this world and that the whole world was his kingdom and thus was good and blessed. God gave the cultural mandate (Gen. 1:26–28) to the human race, which meant that human beings were to use their abilities to care for the world and to develop human culture, thereby releasing the vast potential latent in creation. Their goal in this labor was eternal and eschatological: the new earth. As Plantinga puts it, "we may think of the holy city as the garden of Eden plus the fullness of the centuries."[10]

The fall into sin threatened to destroy this entire project. The fall produced the corruption of every human faculty, all human action, and the created order itself. God, however, not only preserved the world from immediate collapse but also undertook a plan of salvation to ensure that his original purposes for this world are fulfilled. For neo-Calvinism the salvation or redemption brought by Christ is essentially *restoration* or *re-creation*. God does not start over new, but accomplishes his original plan. According to Wolters, our first parents "botched" their original mandate, but God has now given us a "second chance" and has "reinstated" us as his managers on earth.[11] This does not mean that God, through Christ, simply puts us back into the garden of Eden to pick up where Adam left off before he fell. God originally gave Adam the long-term task of unlocking the potentialities of creation through human culture, and despite his sin the human race subsequently has been engaging in that task, though in corrupted form. Redemption in Christ restores and renews human beings in this ongoing task, purging them of their sinful perversion of culture and redirecting them in ways that are obedient to God and beneficial to one another and the whole of creation.[12]

---

[9]Plantinga, *Engaging God's World*, xv. He arranges his chapters around the themes of creation, fall, and redemption. See also Wolters, *Creation Regained*, 10–11, as well as his chapter divisions.

[10]Plantinga, *Engaging God's World*, 33. On this point see also Wolters, *Creation Regained*, 37–41.

[11]Wolters, *Creation Regained*, 11, 57–60.

[12]See ibid., 63–64.

As all of creation and human culture was God's kingdom before the fall, so now the renewal and redemption of all creation in Christ constitute the renewal and redemption of that kingdom. All cultural labor is kingdom work.[13] All cultural labor aims to advance the full realization of that kingdom in the new creation. Our ordinary activity in this world is "kingdom service," which produces "the building materials for that new earth."[14] As Plantinga writes, "What we do now in the name of Christ—striving for healing, for justice, for intellectual light in darkness, striving simply to produce something helpful for sustaining the lives of other human beings—shall be preserved across into the next life."[15]

In light of this grand vision, neo-Calvinism often warns against various "dualistic" views that compromise the holistic character of God's kingdom in this world. Wolters, for example, is very critical of so-called "two-realms" theories that he sees as a perennial danger for Christianity.[16] Wolters rejects any division of life into a "sacred" realm on the one hand, in which people do "kingdom" work, and a "secular" or "profane" realm on the other hand. He fears that Christians holding such a view will depreciate the latter realm or look upon it as inherently inferior. He claims that this view falls prey to a "deep-seated Gnostic tendency." It "restricts the scope of Christ's lordship." Wolters and other neo-Calvinist writers use terms such as "secular" and "profane" to denote things that are inherently evil or at least compromised for the Christian.[17] By rejecting dualistic views, furthermore, neo-Calvinist writers aim to steer Christians away from "vertical" views of salvation that involve "escape" from this world into "heaven," which is the view of Plato rather than Scripture.[18]

---

[13]See Plantinga, *Engaging God's World*, 109–13.

[14]Anthony A. Hoekema, *The Bible and the Future* (Grand Rapids: Eerdmans, 1979), 287.

[15]Plantinga, *Engaging God's World*, 137–38.

[16]Though "two realms" could simply be a synonym for "two kingdoms," and Wolters may have something like this in mind, readers should note that Wolters never specifically addresses a two-kingdoms view such as the one defended in this book.

[17]E.g., see Wolters, *Creation Regained*, 10–11, 53–58, 65, 74; Plantinga, *Engaging God's World*, 96, 123; and Bartholomew and Goheen, *Living at the Crossroads*, 64–65, 135.

[18]E.g., see Bartholomew and Goheen, *Living at the Crossroads*, 52.

N. T. Wright and the New Perspective on Paul

Though neo-Calvinism has been influential in many Reformed and evangelical circles in recent generations, it is far from being the only voice in current discussions about Christianity and culture. As noted, however, many of today's significant voices in the broader Christian world emphasize themes that resemble neo-Calvinist teaching, such as the importance of redemptive cultural transformation and the problem of Platonic and dualistic tendencies in the church. Though there are many theologians and movements that I could mention, I will focus briefly upon two that may be familiar to many readers: the New Perspective on Paul (as represented by N. T. Wright) and the emerging church (as represented by Brian McLaren). As I describe these two, readers should recognize many of the neo-Calvinist themes identified in the previous section.

First I consider the so-called New Perspective on Paul. In the past few decades, this new perspective has sparked discussions about the character of Judaism in Paul's day, Paul's view of Jew-Gentile relations in the early church, his understanding of justification, and his attitude toward the Old Testament law. Proponents of the New Perspective have challenged traditional Protestant readings of Paul that focus upon the universal sinfulness of humanity and God's saving answer to human sin through Christ's atonement, justification, and sanctification. Many recent books address these subjects.[19] Of interest here is what the New Perspective might have to say about Christianity and culture. There is no single set of beliefs that constitute the official New Perspective view on such things. What may be useful is to focus upon the most well-known theologian associated with the New Perspective, Anglican bishop N. T. Wright. One of his recent books, *Surprised by Hope*, has much to

---

[19]Among significant works by New Perspective sympathizers, see N. T. Wright, *What Saint Paul Really Said: Was Paul of Tarsus the Real Founder of Christianity?* (Grand Rapids: Eerdmans, 1997); James D. G. Dunn, *The Theology of Paul the Apostle* (Grand Rapids: Eerdmans, 1998); and N. T. Wright, *Paul: In Fresh Perspective* (Minneapolis: Fortress, 2005). Among significant works critiquing the New Perspective, see Guy Prentiss Waters, *Justification and the New Perspectives on Paul: A Review and Response* (Phillipsburg, NJ: P&R, 2004); and Stephen Westerholm, *Perspectives Old and New on Paul: The "Lutheran" Paul and His Critics* (Grand Rapids: Eerdmans, 2004).

say about Christianity and culture issues. It is remarkable to see how similar his concerns are to those of neo-Calvinist writers such as Wolters and Plantinga.

It is no coincidence that Wright both finds the traditional Reformation view of justification inadequate and also embraces the redemptive transformation of human culture. Before we consider *Surprised by Hope*, let me briefly state a bold claim that I will defend in subsequent chapters. Those who hold a traditional Protestant view of justification *consistently* should not find a redemptive transformationist perspective attractive. As some of the Reformers grasped, a two-kingdoms doctrine is a proper companion to a Protestant doctrine of justification.[20]

Wright is clear about the major theme of *Surprised by Hope*. He sets out to defend the physical resurrection and the physical new heaven and new earth as the great Christian eschatological hope, over against popular misconceptions of Christian hope as "going to heaven" after death, and aims to prove that this hope provides motivation for Christians to transform the present world in anticipation of what is to come.[21] In order to establish and develop this claim, Wright spends considerable time critiquing what he believes is the predominant perspective of the Western church in recent centuries. This perspective emphasizes individual salvation, which consists of our immortal souls being rescued from the present evil world and entering into heaven, a nonmaterial realm that will survive when the present world is completely destroyed at the end of history.[22] According to Wright, such a perspective sounds much more like Plato or Gnosticism than like biblical Christianity.[23] In contrast to this perspective, Wright highlights the resurrection of the dead, which establishes a deep continuity between this present world and the eternal state (though he acknowledges that there is

---

[20]E.g., see John Calvin, *Institutes of the Christian Religion*, 3.19. Also see discussion in David Van-Drunen, "The Two Kingdoms and the *Ordo Salutis*: Life beyond Judgment and the Question of a Dual Ethic," *Westminster Theological Journal* 70 (Fall 2008): 207–24.

[21]See N. T. Wright, *Surprised by Hope: Rethinking Heaven, the Resurrection, and the Mission of the Church* (New York: HarperOne, 2008), 5.

[22]E.g., see ibid., 15, 17, 19, 80, 91, 104–5, 148, 194.

[23]E.g., see ibid., 18, 80, 88–91, 104.

discontinuity too).[24] One significant thing is that believing in the resurrection gives Christians a compelling reason to seek justice and peace in the present world. In contrast, believing in salvation as "going to heaven" to escape this world tends to cause disinterest or indifference to social and cultural affairs.[25]

In order to defend these claims, Wright identifies three grand themes in Scripture: the goodness of God's *creation*, the *evil* in this world due to human rebellion, and God's *redemption* of the world, which consists in God's "liberating" and "remaking" of creation in order to accomplish his original plans for it.[26] Wright's view of the kingdom of God reflects this view of redemption. For Wright, the kingdom has to do not with a future immaterial heaven, but with the present earth as it will be fully renewed in the new creation.[27] Though the coming of the kingdom is ultimately God's work, God enlists the efforts of human beings in bringing the kingdom to final fulfillment. Social transformation in the present is an anticipation of the resurrection and cosmic renewal on the last day.[28] Human beings are "part of the means" by which God brings ultimate salvation, and they are "rescuing stewards over creation." This is the "inner dynamic" of the kingdom of God.[29] At several points Wright refers readers to 1 Corinthians 15:58, with its promise that our work in the Lord is not in vain. From this verse he claims that what we do now is "building for God's kingdom" and "will last into God's future."[30] Though Wright confesses that he has no idea what this will actually look like, he assures Christians: "You are . . . accomplishing something that will become in due course part of God's new world."[31] In light of all this, one of Wright's chief concerns is to reshape his readers' conception of the mission of the church. The church's mission,

[24]E.g., see ibid., 26.
[25]E.g., see ibid., 26–27, 90, 192.
[26]Ibid., 93–97.
[27]E.g., see ibid., 18.
[28]Ibid., 46.
[29]Ibid., 200, 202.
[30]Ibid., 193.
[31]Ibid., 208–9.

he says, should consist not only in evangelism but also in working for justice, peace, and beauty in this present world.[32]

Wright's chief concerns, therefore, closely resemble those of contemporary neo-Calvinism. Over against perceived Platonic tendencies in modern Christianity that despise physical things and devalue cultural activity, both Wright and neo-Calvinists present a creation-fall-redemption perspective that emphasizes the centrality of Christian cultural work as a means of building the kingdom of God and anticipating the new creation.

The Emerging Church

Another contemporary voice that has gained popularity in recent years is that of the "emergent" or "emerging" church.[33] Those involved in the emerging church movement like to emphasize that they are involved in a "conversation" about a new kind of Christianity. They say that this conversation is still ongoing, and so it is hard to predict what exactly this new kind of Christianity will turn out to be. Proponents are critical of traditional forms of Christianity (particularly Reformed and evangelical varieties, from which many of them have come), and have special dislike for rigid doctrine. They are also critical of recent megachurch types of Christianity, in search of something more fresh and authentic. Though it is often unclear what emergent Christianity stands for positively, one thing certainly stands out: its emphasis upon the redemptive transformation of culture as being at the heart of Christian faith. A recent book by leading emergent spokesman Brian McLaren, *Everything Must Change*, provides a good case in point. Though some neo-Calvinists would find McLaren's theology too extreme and might disagree with his left-wing political views, McLaren echoes a great many of their central and standard themes.

This can be seen, first of all, in the forms of Christianity that McLaren combats. McLaren wants to abandon the type of Chris-

---

[32]E.g., see ibid., 193, 212–30.

[33]For two critical descriptions and engagements with emerging Christianity, see David Wells, *The Courage to Be Protestant: Truth-lovers, Marketers, and Emergents in the Postmodern World* (Grand Rapids: Eerdmans, 2008); and Kevin De Young and Ted Kluck, *Why We're Not Emergent: By Two Guys Who Should Be* (Chicago: Moody, 2008).

tianity that proclaims that this sinful world is going to be destroyed and that salvation consists in rescuing "souls" who "escape" from this world and from eternal punishment and are taken to "heaven."[34] Likewise, he opposes "dualistic" Christianity that contrasts the "spiritual" and the "secular" and thus has little interest in social engagement or the current global crisis.[35] In its place, he wants a this-worldly Christianity. He calls for Christians to develop an effective "framing story" (something like a worldview), and the framing story that he defines has nothing to do with Christ's atonement or the forgiveness of sins but everything to do with social "transformation."[36] His framing story affirms that Jesus came to "retrain and restore humanity to its original vocation and potential. This renewed humanity can return to its role as caretakers of creation and one another so the planet and all it contains can be restored to the healthy and fruitful harmony that God desires."[37] Thus Jesus proclaimed the kingdom of God not in terms of escaping from this world but "in terms of God's dream coming true for this earth, of God's justice and peace replacing earth's injustice and disharmony."[38] Not unexpectedly, McLaren sees the vision of the New Jerusalem in Revelation 21 as providing "hope within history," which means that this vision "seeks to inspire our imaginations with hope about what our world can actually become." It shows "a new way of living that is possible within this universe, a new societal system that is coming as surely as God is just and faithful."[39] The gospel of the kingdom of God, therefore, is about our work of transforming the world toward peace and justice, and the New Jerusalem is the result of this process.

The Two-Kingdoms Alternative

A person can learn some very important things about Christianity and the Christian's cultural responsibilities by reading neo-Calvinist,

---

[34]McLaren, *Everything Must Change*, 3–4, 18–19, 77–80, and elsewhere.

[35]E.g., see ibid., 81–83.

[36]E.g., see ibid., chap. 9 generally (and 72–73 especially). Talk of "transformation" occurs repeatedly throughout this book.

[37]Ibid., 129.

[38]Ibid., 21.

[39]Ibid., 296.

New Perspective, and emerging authors. The physical created world is God's good creation, sin is a horrible and distorting thing, God has not given up on his original goal for creation, cultural vocations are honorable and beneficial, Christians should think critically about sin's effects upon cultural life, and the resurrection and the new heaven and new earth are the great Christian hope. The problem is, I believe, that these authors quite confidently give the impression that their visions of cultural transformation, the kingdom of God, and the new creation are the only way to affirm these things. They suggest that the only people who would oppose their vision are those who are indifferent to the broader culture, reject the resurrection, and hope only to escape to heaven where they will float around as happy spirits. This is a terribly distorted and misleading suggestion. Great Christian leaders such as Augustine, Luther, and Calvin—to name but a few—respected earthly vocations and affirmed the resurrection of the dead. But they also made very clear that the Christian's cultural activities have to be carefully distinguished from the coming of the kingdom and the hope of the new creation. Such distinctions, they believed, were crucial to Christian faith and life.[40]

This book, in developing a contemporary and biblically-based two-kingdoms doctrine, follows this Augustinian and Reformation trajectory. Though I present an approach to Christianity and culture that is different from the transformationist visions exemplified by neo-Calvinism, Wright, and McLaren, readers should expect to find a defense of classic Christian doctrines such as creation, the fall, and the resurrection within these pages. Likewise, readers should not expect to find any hostility or indifference toward the broader world of human culture. I confess to loving many cultural activities. I am a proficient pianist and organist, read novels and *The Wall Street Journal* nearly every day, love college football, am an attorney (though currently on inactive status, so please don't call for legal advice), and play golf to a low handicap (you certainly may call if

---

[40]See the discussion in VanDrunen, *Natural Law and the Two Kingdoms*, chaps. 2–3. Among important primary sources discussed there, see book 19 of Augustine's *City of God*, Luther's famous treatise, "Temporal Authority: To What Extent It Should Be Obeyed," and sections 3.19.15–16 and 4.20.1 of Calvin's *Institutes*.

you are a member of a nice club and wish to invite me for a round). What readers can expect to find in this book is a positive view of cultural activity—though a positive view that is also reserved. It is reserved because it seeks to follow Scripture's teaching that the affairs of human culture are temporary, provisional, and bound to pass away. The kingdom of God proclaimed by the Lord Jesus Christ is *not* built through politics, commerce, music, or sports. Redemption does not consist in restoring people to fulfill Adam's original task, but consists in the Lord Jesus Christ himself fulfilling Adam's original task once and for all, on our behalf. Thus redemption is not "creation regained" but "re-creation gained." What readers can expect to find in this book most of all, therefore, is a high view of the Lord Jesus Christ, his perfect redeeming work, and his eternal kingdom—a kingdom advancing now through the ministry and life of the church and one day to be revealed in consummate glory apart from any work of our own human culture. This kingdom, proclaimed by Christ, deserves a defense in the present day, and this book, however humbly, seeks to provide one.

In short, Scripture requires a high view of creation and of cultural activity, but it also requires a distinction between the holy things of Christ's heavenly kingdom and the common things of the present world. It requires a distinction between God's providential sustaining of human culture for the whole of the human race and his glorious redemption of a chosen people that he has gathered into a church now and will gather into the new creation for eternity. Some people indeed fall into unwarranted "dualisms," but dualism-phobia must not override our ability to make clear and necessary *distinctions*. Some people indeed are guilty of promoting a godless and amoral "secular" realm, but the fear of a godless secularism should not eliminate our ability to speak of a *divinely-ordained common* kingdom that is legitimate but not holy.[41] The two-kingdoms doctrine

---

[41] It could be appropriate to use the word "secular" to describe the common kingdom. "Secular" does not have to be a bad word. The Latin word *saeculum* simply means "an age," and many writers—including Christian writers—use the term "secular" to refer to the affairs of this present world (in comparison to the affairs of the world to come following Christ's return). In this sense I think a limited use of the word "secular" can be helpful, though I avoid using the term in this book due to possible misunderstanding.

enables us to affirm the goodness of creation and culture without losing sight of crucial distinctions. The two-kingdoms doctrine helps us to account for the whole biblical story.·

In presenting this two-kingdoms vision, I hope to provide encouragement to ordinary Christians—to ordinary Christians who work, study, vote, raise families, help the poor, run businesses, make music, watch movies, ride bikes, and engage in all sorts of other cultural activities, and who wish to live thoughtful and God-pleasing lives in doing so. I hope that this book will be an encouragement for many readers to take up their many cultural activities with renewed vigor, being convinced that such activities are good and pleasing to God. For many readers I also hope that this book will be liberating, freeing you from well-meaning but nonbiblical pressure from other Christians to "transform" your workplace or to find uniquely "Christian" ways of doing ordinary tasks. For all readers I hope that this book will serve to focus your hearts on things that are far more important than a promotion at work or the most recent Supreme Court decision: the sufficiency of the work of Christ, the missionary task of the church, and the hope of the new heaven and new earth.

The Plan of This Book

In order to give readers an initial taste of what this two-kingdoms doctrine is, how it fits into the grand sweep of biblical history, and why it is so eminently practical for daily Christian life, I now briefly describe the argument of this book and how it unfolds in the following chapters. Whenever we begin to examine an unfamiliar idea, it is helpful to get a sense of the big picture. Hence, in part 1, I set the camera lens at its widest possible angle, looking at the question of human culture by means of Paul's description of the two Adams that stride across all of history. The first Adam is of course the original human person described in the early chapters of Genesis, and I focus upon him in chapter 2. God created Adam and Eve in his image and gave them a task to accomplish: to be fruitful and multiply and to exercise dominion over the earth. At the dawn of history, therefore, God gave a *cultural* task to the human race. What is more, God set a goal and reward before the first Adam. If he completed his cultural task through faithful obedience to God's commands, God would have brought Adam into a new creation (what the New Testament calls the "world to come" or "the new heaven and new earth") far surpassing the delightful and sinless world into which Adam was originally created. By a divine covenant, Adam's righteous cultural labors would have earned him a share in the eschatological world-to-come. Instead, Adam fell into sin and plunged the present world into a state of sin and misery.

The first Adam failed terribly, but God sent a second and last Adam into the world, the Lord Jesus Christ. Chapter 3 tells the main points of this wonderful biblical story. Christ the last Adam not only took upon himself the penalty of the first Adam's sin, but also took upon himself the responsibility of fulfilling Adam's original task. Christ offered perfect obedience in this world to his Father, and was exalted to his right hand as a result. The Lord Jesus, as a human being—as the last Adam—has attained the original goal held out for Adam: a glorified life ruling the world-to-come. Because Jesus has fulfilled the first Adam's commission, those who belong to Christ by faith are no longer given that commission. Christians already possess eternal life and claim an everlasting inheritance. God does not call them to engage in cultural labors so as to earn their place in the world-to-come. We are not little Adams. Instead, God gives us a share in the world-to-come as a gift of free grace in Christ and then calls us to live obediently in this world as a grateful response. Our cultural activities do not in any sense usher in the new creation. The new creation has been earned and attained once and for all by Christ, the last Adam. Cultural activity remains important for Christians, but it will come to an abrupt end, along with this present world as a whole, when Christ returns and cataclysmically ushers in the new heaven and new earth.

After part 1 provides this big-picture view of human culture in the biblical story, part 2 examines the same topic but with a more detailed examination of the experience of God's people between the fall of Adam and the second coming of Christ. In chapter 4 I trace this story through the Old Testament. Immediately after the fall into sin, God placed enmity between the seed of the woman and the seed of Satan. Not only did God promise a Savior who would overturn the effects of the fall, but he also decreed that there would be a deep-seated conflict between those who belong to him by faith and those who remain enslaved to Satan. A fundamental *antithesis* exists between believer and unbeliever in their basic perspective and attitude toward God, morality, and eternity, and this antithesis manifested itself clearly in the story of Cain and Abel. But alongside this antithesis God also ordained an element of *commonality* in the world. The antithesis between belief and unbelief would often not be evident to the naked eye. Believers and unbelievers would share many things in common and work together in many areas of cultural life (despite their fundamental disagreements about the most important things). Unbelievers would even surpass believers in many cultural pursuits. In this dual reality of antithesis and commonality lies the origin of the two kingdoms. Early in Genesis God established two covenants, by which the two kingdoms were formally established. In his covenant with Noah God entered covenantal relationship with the entire human race (and with the entire creation), promising to preserve its cultural activities such as procreating and securing justice. This was the formal establishment of the "common kingdom." In his covenant with Abraham, in contrast, God entered covenantal relationship with a chosen people, upon whom he bestows eternal salvation by faith, thereby distinguishing them from the rest of the human race. This was the formal establishment of the "redemptive kingdom." God's people are thus called to live under both covenants—that is, in two kingdoms. On the one hand, they respect the terms of the Noahic covenant as they pursue a variety of cultural activities in common with unbelievers. On the other hand, they embrace the terms of the Abrahamic covenant of grace as they cling to the promises of salvation and eternal life in a new creation and as they gather in worshiping communities distinguished from the unbelieving world. The experiences of Abraham and of the Israelite exiles in Babylon (though not of Israel in the Promised Land) especially exemplify the two-kingdoms way of life in the Old Testament.

Chapter 5 continues to chart this story as it unfolds in the New Testament. Through the coming of Christ and his life, death, resurrection, and ascension, the promises of God came to fulfillment. The last Adam took away the sins of his people, fulfilled God's law in their place (as the first Adam should have done), and entered into the world-to-come, attaining the original human destiny. He announced the coming of his kingdom during his earthly ministry and is now gathering his people into a worldwide church to enjoy the fellowship of that kingdom in the present age. The New Testament thus presents God's people as standing on the very brink of eternity, at the cusp of the new creation. But it also speaks of the present time as one of suffering and uses terms such as "exile," "alien," and "sojourner" to describe Christians, thus recollecting the days of Abraham and the Babylonian captivity. Christians live under two kingdoms, governed respectively by the Noahic covenant and the Abrahamic covenant. Civil governments, families, economic associations, and many other cultural institutions continue to exist under the covenant with Noah, and Christians and non-Christians alike participate in them and, in many respects, cooperate in their activities. At Christ's return these institutions and activities will come to a sudden and radical end. Yet Christians belong especially to the church, the New Testament manifestation of the special covenant community created in Abraham. Through the church they are citizens of heaven even now. This church—God's redemptive kingdom in the present age—has a distinct membership, faith, worship, and ethic. Its way of life displays a counterculture to the cultures of this world. The church awaits the coming of Christ as a day of glorious consummation, when the bride will see her bridegroom face-to-face as she is ushered into the wedding banquet of the Lamb.

Finally, in part 3 I turn to some concrete, practical issues that explore the implications of living the Christian life in two kingdoms. First, chapter 6 addresses the church as the present manifestation of the redemptive kingdom. Here I defend the claim that the life and ministry of the church—rather than the cultural life and activities of the common kingdom—stand at the heart of the Christian life. Especially through its worship and celebration of the Lord's

Day, the church experiences a foretaste of the new creation in the present world. In all sorts of ways the church has a culture distinct from the cultures of the common kingdom. Unlike the institutions of the common kingdom, the church lives by an ethic of forgiveness that transcends the claims of justice, by an ethic of generosity that defies the scarcity of economic resources, and by a missionary evangelism that shuns coercion. The church attends to the business of the redemptive kingdom and does not trample on the authority of common kingdom institutions. Unlike these other institutions, its authority derives from the Scriptures *alone*.

The final chapter, chapter 7, continues this discussion of the practical implications of the two-kingdoms doctrine for the Christian life. I reflect upon three important and controversial areas of culture: education, work, and politics. Scripture speaks about all of these activities and thus provides Christians with a proper perspective on them and clear boundaries for participating in them. But Scripture addresses these issues only in a broad and general way. Christians are always obligated to follow Scripture's instructions about these activities, but where Scripture is silent Christians must exercise their own wisdom to make godly decisions in concrete circumstances. Furthermore, though education, work, and politics are distinct activities that require their own separate analysis, they all involve the life of the common kingdom under the Noahic covenant and require Christians, to some degree or another, to work alongside unbelievers in pursuing them. Learning, working, and voting are not uniquely Christian tasks, but common tasks. Christians should always be distinguished from unbelievers *subjectively*: they do all things by faith in Christ and for his glory. But as an *objective* matter, the standards of morality and excellence in the common kingdom are ordinarily the same for believers and unbelievers: they share these standards in common under God's authority in the covenant with Noah.

That, in summary, is the plan of this book. May God be honored in this account of his ways of dealing with this world. May his people be encouraged, as they pursue their cultural tasks with wisdom and excellence, ever more to trust in Christ's all-sufficient work, to revel in the church as a foretaste of the kingdom of heaven in an evil age, and to look forward with eager hearts to the dawn of a new age, when Christ returns and the new heaven and new earth are revealed in all their glory.

A Note about the Term "Culture"

Terminology can be tricky. I have already, in footnotes, discussed loaded terms such as "transformation" and "secular" that have a variety of connotations and are used in different ways. As far as possible I want this book to be about substantive ideas rather than about terminology, and thus it is important to clarify my use of certain terms that may provoke misunderstanding. Two such terms that I use throughout this book are "culture" and "cultural."

In a broad sense, culture refers to all of the various human activities and their products, as well as the way in which we interpret them and the language we use to describe them. Interpretation and language, as well as the products themselves, are crucial parts of culture because the same product can serve very different functions in different contexts.[42] In this broad sense of culture, practically everything we do is "cultural," whether activities of high culture or popular culture, or mundane tasks like brushing our teeth. Not only nation-states but also neighborhoods, universities, athletic leagues, families, churches, and all sorts of other things have their own cultures, which are often overlapping. In a book such as this, I do not use the term "culture" in an overly precise or technical way. I use it primarily to refer to the broad range of activities—scientific, artistic, economic, etc.—in which human beings engage. The popular expression, "Christianity and culture," which appears in the subtitle of this book, simply refers to the variety of questions that emerge when we consider how Christians and the church are to relate to these broad activities of human culture and how Christian faith affects our interpretation of them.

---

[42]For helpful thoughts on what "culture" is, in the context of two-kingdoms and neo-Calvinist paradigms relevant to this book, see Ryan McIlhenny, "A Third-Way Reformed Approach to Christ and Culture: Appropriating Kuyperian Neocalvinism and the Two Kingdoms Perspective," *Mid-America Journal of Theology* 20 (2009): 75–94

FIRST THINGS AND LAST THINGS

Have you ever seen a book that you knew nothing about, taken it off the shelf, opened it up to a random page, and read the first paragraph that your eyes happened to meet? Depending on the book, you may have been intrigued, or offended, or amused. But one thing is almost certain—you did not fully understand that paragraph. No matter how clearly the paragraph was written, you did not fully understand it because you read it in isolation, apart from its larger context. If the book was a novel, you did not know who the characters were or how the plot had developed to that point. If the book was a scholarly work making a careful argument for a controversial claim, you did not know what the author's claim was or what the initial steps of his argument were. To understand *part* of a book well, in other words, we must understand something about the book as a *whole*.

It is no different with reading the Bible. The Bible is a very big book, written by many human authors, in several different languages, with a variety of literary styles, over more than a thousand years. Many of the individual parts of the Bible are very hard to understand and some of them even seem to contradict each other at first reading. Yet Christians believe that there is also one divine author of Scripture and that therefore the parts of Scripture are not contradictory but fit together into a single, unified story that proclaims the truth about God and his relationship with the world. In order to understand what Scripture teaches about any subject, we must appreciate both the particular things that it says about it at various places in the text and how those particular things fit into the larger story and unified truth that the Bible communicates.

These considerations should guide our reflection on the Christian's relationship to human culture. Part 1 of this book considers some very big issues that provide the basics for thinking about Christianity and cultural activity. Many contemporary writers portray redemption as "creation regained," as picking up Adam's original task of developing culture with the goal of adorning the new creation, all so that God's original plans for this world might be fulfilled. In part 1 we will see that God's original plan for creation is indeed fulfilled—but *not* through the cultural works of Christians. The Lord Jesus Christ, as the second and last Adam, has fulfilled Adam's original commission once and for all. Christ has already attained the original goal by entering the new creation through his resurrection and ascension. And we already have a claim to this new creation by virtue of his work. We are citizens of heaven through faith in him.

This is crucial background for the rest of the book. If we do not understand the biblical theme of the two Adams and its corresponding doctrine of justification then it is impossible to hold a biblical view of Christianity and culture. Readers who think that Christianity is about picking up Adam's original task and doing it better than he did should probably hold a redemptive transformationist view and proceed as if their cultural achievements will adorn the new heaven and new earth. But if you follow the discussion in chapters 2 and 3 about the two Adams—the first Adam and the last Adam, in Paul's language—then you have the foundation for understanding the development and importance of the two kingdoms through the grand story of biblical history.

The First Adam

Creation and Fall

PAUL'S EPISTLE TO THE ROMANS has long held a special and well-deserved place in the hearts of Protestant Christians. Like no other biblical book, Romans unfolds the devastation of human sin, the inescapability of God's judgment, the amazing gift of salvation, the outlook for the eschatological future, and the character of the Christian life. About one-third of the way through the book, in 5:12–21, Paul brings a key argument of Romans to a dramatic climax before moving on to the next stage of his epistle. In these verses Paul repeatedly compares "one man" with "one man." The first man, he explains, committed "one trespass" which "led to condemnation for all men" while the second man performed "one act of righteousness" that "leads to justification and life for all men" (5:18). Because of the first man's "disobedience" the "many were made sinners," but by the second man's "obedience the many will be made righteous" (5:19). Two great figures, Adam and Christ, overshadow the whole of human history. The fate of every other individual depends upon the two of them.

This was no slip of Paul's pen. The same theme appears in 1 Corinthians: "For as by a man came death, by a man has come also the resurrection of the dead. For as in Adam all die, so also in Christ shall all be made alive" (15:21–22). Later Paul adds: "Thus it is written, 'The first man Adam became a living being'; the last Adam became a life-giving spirit. . . . Just as we have borne the image of the man of dust, we shall also bear the image of the man of heaven" (15:45, 49).

Two Adams stand over the whole of human history. The first Adam was the pinnacle of God's original creation and held the destiny of the world in his hands. By his disobedience the world was plunged into sin, condemnation, and death. But the second and last Adam came from heaven into the midst of this fallen world, fulfilled the task of the first Adam, endured the death and judgment due to sin, and entered into the new creation by his resurrection and ascension.

There is no better way to summarize the story of Scripture, and hence the story of world history. Christians must understand their responsibilities in human culture within the context of this bigger story. Redemption is not about regaining the original creation but gaining the new creation by the work of Christ alone. Christians' cultural activities should not be construed as picking up Adam's original task. This chapter describes the opening part of the story, creation and fall, as it revolves around the first Adam.

The Creation of the World

Athletic events and musical performances generally begin with a warm-up. Athletes need to get their hearts beating and their muscles limber. Musicians need to loosen their fingers, lips, or vocal cords. But Scripture does not begin slowly. Genesis 1 is no warm-up, but begins with an astounding account of God's work of creation that, in a beautiful literary style, describes the origin of all things, the ordering of this world's many parts into a harmonious whole, and the climactic act of human creation in the divine image.

Many features of Genesis 1 are striking, especially when compared with the creation myths of many ancient peoples. Genesis 1 reveals that there is but one God, not a pantheon of gods who will share the work and compete for the glory. This one God, furthermore, was the only being who existed before creation. In the beginning God created "the heavens and the earth"—everything owes its existence to God's creative power. As the New Testament puts it, "the universe was created by the word of God, so that what is seen was not made out of things that are visible" (Heb. 11:3). Thus, unlike many creation myths, there was no one or no thing that opposed God when he created. Another striking feature of Genesis 1 is the almighty power of God. Nothing is difficult for God, nothing is a struggle. He simply speaks, and whatever he says comes to pass. The psalmist later comments: "By the word of the LORD the heavens were made, and by the breath of his mouth all their host" (Ps. 33:6). Finally, Genesis 1 highlights the unadulterated goodness of God's work. Six times this chapter says that God looked at what he had created and saw that "it was good." Then, after creating man last of all, "God saw everything that he had made, and behold, it was very good" (1:31).

It is no wonder that the rest of Scripture looks back upon the work of creation and marvels at such a God. "O LORD, how manifold are your works! In wisdom have you made them all; the earth is full of your creatures" (Ps. 104:24). Even in the final book of Scripture the wonder of creation continues to amaze the heavenly host: "Worthy are you, our Lord and God, to receive glory and honor and power, for you created all things, and by your will they existed and were created" (Rev. 4:11).

While we are admiring the work of God described in Genesis 1, we do well to peek ahead for a moment to the opening of Genesis 2. There we see a curious thing, but something that is immensely important for understanding Christianity and culture today: a seventh day on which God does no creating at all. Genesis 1:31–2:1 explains that in the work of the six days God made "everything" and thus the heavens and earth were "finished." But then on the seventh day God "rested ... from all his work that he had done" and "blessed the seventh day and made it holy" (2:2–3). God sits down, as it were, enthroned above the world that he has made, rejoicing in his accomplishment. For six days God acted again and again in this world, but on the seventh day he withdraws his hand of creation from the world and takes up his royal rest in the heavens above.

It is evident that the main actor in Genesis 1 is God himself. He is front and center. But within the created world one creature stands out from all the rest: "man," whom God made "male and female" (Gen. 1:26–27). Every other creature clearly has its place and contributes in its own wonderful way to the glory of the Lord. But Genesis 1 tells us about the creation of all other beings before it gets to the creation of human beings, and with this climactic act its story of creation is complete. Several aspects of Genesis 1 indicate that the creation of human beings is unique. For example, on several occasions God calls upon things that he has already made to assist him in the production of other things: "Let the earth sprout. . . . Let the waters swarm. . . . Let the earth bring forth . . ." (1:11, 20, 24). But when it comes time to make human beings the language changes: "Let us make man . . ." (1:26). Furthermore, on several occasions God speaks creatures into existence "according to their kinds" (1:11–12, 21, 24–25). But when he makes man he creates them "in our image, after our likeness" (1:26).

Bearing the image and likeness of God is the thing that sets apart human beings from the rest of creation most clearly and dramatically. What did it mean for the first Adam to be created in God's image? Ephesians 4:24 and Colossians 3:10 provide some clues about how to read Genesis 1:26–27. In these two verses Paul writes about the Christian's *renewal* in the image of God through faith in Christ, thereby indicating that the image of God in Christ is not something entirely new but reflects the image as originally created by God. So what does Paul say about the image? He speaks of it in terms of "knowledge" (Col. 3:10) and "righteousness and holiness" (Eph. 4:24). Knowledge, righteousness, and holiness refer to moral and rational capabilities *put to good use.* Thus Paul indicates that bearing God's image is about *who we are* and especially *what we do.*

Back in Genesis 1 we find exactly what Paul's words lead us to expect. For many nonhuman things, such as the expanse in the midst of the waters and the lights in the heavens (1:6, 14), what God made them to *be* is inseparable from what he made them to *do*.[1] The same is evidently true for Adam. God made the first Adam a moral and rational creature who must put these capacities to work. Unlike all the other creatures, Adam can hear and understand God's words, is put under obligation, and must render account to God. What exactly were Adam and Eve to do as knowledgeable, righteous, and holy creatures? Genesis 1:26 explains: "let them have dominion over the fish of the sea and over the birds of the heavens and over the livestock and over all the earth and over every creeping thing that creeps on the earth." Exercising dominion was not something tacked on to image-bearing: to exercise dominion is part of the very nature of bearing the image.[2] Genesis 1:1–25 reveals a God who has exercised supreme dominion over this world, calling it into being, ordering its various parts, and giving names to his creatures. Then he creates man in his image and *likeness*—what could be more *like God* than exercising dominion in the world? This dominion must be exercised, of course, under the sovereign dominion of God. The first Adam is an under-lord serving the supreme Lord. But in carrying out this responsibility he shows forth the likeness of his Creator in a way that far surpasses the work of any other creature.

In other words, to bear the image of God was to be entrusted with an office or a commission. God made Adam to be a wise, holy, and righteous *king*. He was to pick up where God left off. God named many created things (1:5, 8, 10), but he commissioned Adam to name many that he had not named (2:19–20). God brought the first human

---

[1]For discussion of this important point, see, e.g., David J. A. Clines, "Humanity as the Image of God," in *On the Way to the Postmodern: Old Testament Essays, 1967–1998*, vol. 2 (Sheffield: Sheffield Academic Press, 1998), 490–92; Phyllis A. Bird, " 'Male and Female He Created Them': Gen 1:27b in the Context of the Priestly Account of Creation, *Harvard Theological Review* 74.2 (1981): 138; and J. Richard Middleton, *The Liberating Image: The* Imago Dei *in Genesis 1* (Grand Rapids: Brazos, 2005), 53–54.

[2]The grammar of the original Hebrew text likely indicates that there is a purpose clause in Genesis 1:26, such that we might translate it as follows: "Let us make man in our image, after our likeness, *so that they might* have dominion. . . ." E.g., see Paul Joüon, S. J., *A Grammar of Biblical Hebrew*, trans. and rev. T. Muraoka (Rome: Editrice Pontificio Instituto Biblico, 1991), 2:381, who sees here an indirect volitive indicating purpose. Bruce K. Waltke and M. O'Connor present a different view of the grammar in *An Introduction to Biblical Hebrew Syntax* (Winona Lake: Eisenbrauns, 1990), 653–54. They see here not an indirect volitive but a conjunctive *waw*, joining two clauses "not otherwise logically related."

beings to life, but he commissioned Adam and Eve to populate the world with a multitude of descendants (1:28). God made Adam with a host of latent abilities that he was to develop and put to use in benevolent rule over all other living beings (1:26, 28). Hence, we see already in the first chapter of Scripture that human beings were made for *cultural* activity. God gave to them a cultural task that they were to pursue in faithful service to him. Telling the biblical story of Christianity and culture must begin in Genesis 1.

A good summary of the image of God thus far may be something like this: the first Adam was made in the divine image as *the royal son of God, commissioned to exercise wise, righteous, and holy dominion over this world.*

But there is still one thing missing in this definition of the image. The conclusion of the creation narrative, Genesis 2:1–3, teaches that after God finished his work he sat down enthroned in the heavens in royal rest. God worked—and then he rested. If the first Adam was made in God's image and likeness, and was commissioned to work as God had worked, was he also to rest as God had rested? Was the image of God not only about working (and working and working and working . . .) but also about *finishing* the work and *resting* like God himself? Genesis 1:1–2:3 does not exactly say it, but it leads us to suspect that this is the case. Other places in Scripture confirm this suspicion and show us how important it is. The first Adam did not bear God's image in order to work aimlessly in the original creation but to finish his work in this world and then to enter a new creation and to sit down enthroned in a royal rest.

Human Destiny: Ruling the World-to-Come

I have just described the original *human destiny*. The so-called "cultural mandate" of Genesis 1:26, 28 was not a task of infinite duration. The human race was to complete its task in this world and then to enter triumphantly into the world-to-come. Hebrews 2:5 describes this destiny: "Now it was not to angels that God subjected the world to come, of which we are speaking." The following verses quote from Psalm 8 to show that God subjected the world-to-come not to angels but to *human beings*: "What is man, that you are mindful of him, or the son of man, that you care for him? You made him for a little while lower than the angels; you have crowned him with glory and honor, putting everything in subjection under his feet." Note that Psalm 8 refers to the *original creation*. From the beginning, *even before the fall into sin*, God destined human beings to be rulers over all things, ultimately in a "world to come." Hebrews 4:1–10 identifies this human destiny in the world-to-come (now accomplished in Christ) as a participation in God's seventh-day rest of Genesis 2:1–3.

Hebrews 2:5–8, therefore, confirms our suspicion about Genesis 2:1–3. As an image-bearer of God, the first Adam was not only to pursue cultural activity in this world but was also to enter the world-to-come. He was not only to be like God in exercising royal dominion in the original creation, but was to enter into a royal rest as ruler of the new creation. He was to follow the pattern of his God, who did magnificent work in this world for six days and then sat down enthroned on the seventh day. He could look forward to partaking of the tree of life (Gen. 2:9), which was not the symbol of life upon this earth, but of life in a new heavens and new earth (Rev. 22:2).

Now we might wonder what would have happened to the rest of us if Adam had successfully completed the task that God gave him. Romans 5:12–19 explains that Adam was acting on behalf of the whole human race. The first Adam was the *representative* of us all, and the consequences of Adam's actions have fallen upon his posterity. Scripture does not tell us exactly how things would have unfolded, but if the first Adam had been obedient then the rest of us would still have come into existence and shared the glory of the world-to-come with him in the presence of God.

But how would it be determined when Adam had done enough and had "finished his work" as God had finished his (2:2)? Genesis 2 provides the answer. In Genesis 1:26–28 God gave Adam broad commands, with the whole world in view, but in Genesis 2:15–17 God gives Adam more specific commands, with a particular location, the garden of Eden, in view. He puts Adam in the garden, instructs him "to work it and keep it," and then commands him not to eat of the tree of the knowledge of good and evil, lest he die. Many features of the biblical text indicate that the garden of Eden was a temple.[3] The whole world belonged to God, but Eden was the place of his special holy dwelling. In Eden God puts Adam to the test and will find out whether he is a faithful image-bearer who should reign in the world-to-come or an unfaithful image-bearer who must die.

A careful look at Genesis 2:15 displays how Adam's general obligations of Genesis 1 are put to a specific and focused test in Genesis 2. While Genesis 1:26–28 requires Adam to serve as a king, Genesis 2:15 requires Adam to serve as a king and also as a priest. Some writers point to the contemporary cultural relevance of Genesis 2:15 by interpreting the command to "work" the garden as a requirement to develop the potential of the creation through human civilization and interpreting the command to "keep" (or "care for") the garden as a requirement to be ecologically sensitive.[4] Adam probably was called to cultivate the garden in productive ways as part of his royal dominion, and undoubtedly he was to be environmentally responsible, but the main point of Genesis 2:15 is that Adam's royal dominion was also to be priestly service. For one thing, as noted, the garden of Eden is a temple, and temples are the place where priests do their work. Furthermore, when the Hebrew words "work" and "keep" are used together in the Old Testament, they ordinarily refer to priestly labor. In fact, the term "keep" is often used in the Old Testament to describe the obligation of priests to *guard* the holy tabernacle (and this is precisely the term used in Genesis 3:24 to describe the cherubim who "guard" the way back into Eden after Adam and Eve sin). God's command

---

[3]For biblical evidence see G. K. Beale, *The Temple and the Church's Mission: A Biblical Theology of the Dwelling Place of God* (Downers Grove: InterVarsity, 2004), 70–76. At the end of Scripture the apostle John sees the "new heaven and new earth" (Rev. 21:1), but then focuses upon the New Jerusalem, which he describes as both a city and a temple, through the rest of Revelation 21–22; see Beale, *The Temple and the Church's Mission*, 23–25. At the beginning of Scripture, similarly, Genesis initially describes the creation of "the first heaven and the first earth" (see Rev. 21:1) and Adam and Eve's obligation to rule the whole world (Genesis 1) but then focuses upon one spot on the earth in Genesis 2:8–25.

[4]E.g., see Michael W. Goheen and Craig G. Bartholomew, *Living at the Crossroads: An Introduction to Christian Worldview* (Grand Rapids: Brazos, 2008), 44–45.

to "keep" the garden was really a command to guard it against anything that would defile it.[5]

Adam's royal task of Genesis 1 and his royal-priestly task of Genesis 2 were therefore inseparable. Adam was obliged to exercise dominion over all the other creatures (1:26, 28) and to guard the garden (2:15), so if any creature would seek to usurp authority and threaten the holiness of the garden (which is precisely what the serpent did in Genesis 3), then Adam would have to obey God's commands in Genesis 1:26, 28 through obeying his commands in Genesis 2:15: he would have to assert his authority over this creature and protect the garden's purity. Thus God was going to bring Adam's obligations into focus and test his obedience. Would he obey God? Would he be a faithful king under God's authority? Would he protect the purity of God's holy presence from anything that might defile it? Adam's probation in Eden would determine the answers.

In Reformed theology this relationship between God and the first Adam is referred to as a *covenant* (called specifically the covenant of creation, or the covenant of works, or the covenant of life).[6] Though the word "covenant" does not appear in Genesis 1–2, there is good reason to use this terminology.[7] The idea of a covenant between God and the first Adam at creation nicely summarizes the things that we have seen up to this point: God entered into a covenant with Adam, promising him eternal life in glory if he obeyed his commission and threatening him with death if he disobeyed. How would human history turn out, in light of this momentous responsibility placed upon Adam's shoulders?

---

[5]See discussion, e.g., in Bryan D. Estelle, "The Covenant of Works in Moses and Paul," in *Covenant, Justification, and Pastoral Ministry: Essays by the Faculty of Westminster Seminary California*, ed. R. Scott Clark (Phillipsburg, NJ: P&R, 2007), 100–02; and in Beale, *The Temple and the Church's Mission*, 66–69, 84–85, 87. For later biblical instruction to priests commanding them to "guard" the tabernacle, see Numbers 3:6–7, 32, 38; 18:1–7.

[6]A brief, classic statement of the Reformed view of this original covenant is found in the Westminster Confession of Faith 7.2: "The first covenant made with man was a covenant of works, wherein life was promised to Adam; and in him to his posterity, upon condition of perfect and personal obedience."

[7]For a recent brief defense, see e.g., see J. V. Fesko, *Justification: Understanding the Classic Reformed Doctrine* (Phillipsburg, NJ: P&R, 2008), 108–22.

The Fall: Condemnation, Depravity, and Death

We know all too well how Adam did. After explaining that God destined *human beings* to rule the world-to-come, Hebrews 2 goes on to say, with understated but devastating accuracy, "At present, we do not yet see everything in subjection to him" (2:8). Indeed we do not seem like the kind of creatures meant to be the kings of a new creation. We have a hard enough time keeping order amongst ourselves. The natural forces of disease, drought, flood, wildfire, hurricane, earthquake, tsunami, and tornado remain largely out of our control. The author of Hebrews wants us to ponder a pitiful truth. God destined us to rule the world-to-come, and look at how inept we are dealing with the present world!

Genesis 3 describes what happened. It introduces a new character, "the serpent," whom Scripture later identifies as the devil (Rev. 12:9; 20:2). He begins talking to Eve and with great subtlety twists God's words and challenges his goodness. Within five short verses the serpent has deceived Eve and persuaded her to eat from the tree of the knowledge of good and evil (without ever directly telling her to do so), and she in turn gives the fruit to Adam, who eats too (3:6).

Genesis 3 confirms that Adam's general commission to exercise royal dominion was to focus specifically on the garden and would be tested through the tree of the knowledge of good and evil. It clarifies that the command about the tree (2:16–17) was *not* simply an arbitrary requirement unrelated to Adam's general obligation to exercise dominion (1:26, 28). The tree of the knowledge of good and evil did not test Adam's willingness to obey an arbitrary divine command, but tested how faithfully he would exercise dominion by guarding the purity of the holy garden. The serpent came not simply as a tempter but as an *intruder* who threatened to defile God's temple. Adam was with Eve when the serpent tempted her (3:6). Would he, as a loyal king and priest, rule over the serpent and expel him from the garden, or would he let the serpent rule over him and pollute the garden? When Adam stood by idly while the serpent worked his mischief and then joined Eve in her rebellion, he did not simply disobey the command not to eat from this tree (2:16–17). He also disobeyed the dominion mandate of 1:26, 28—he abdicated his kingship and allowed the serpent to be king of God's creation. And he also disobeyed the command in 2:15 to work and guard the garden—he despised his priesthood and allowed the serpent to defile what he should have kept pure.[8]

God's judgments against Adam and Eve later in Genesis 3 strike exactly at the points where God had demanded obedience. In the curse upon the woman, for example, God states: "I will surely multiply your pain in childbearing; in pain you shall bring forth children" (3:16). This curse falls upon one of the primary activities—being fruitful and multiplying—that was to characterize human dominion over this world (1:28). God also pronounces a curse upon the man: "cursed is the ground because of you; in pain you shall eat of it all the days of your life; thorns and thistles it shall bring forth for you; and you shall eat the plants of the field. By the sweat of your face you shall eat bread . . ." (3:17–19). This curse falls upon another activity that was to characterize human dominion: the command to "work and keep" the garden (2:15). Adam was to be lord of the land and guardian of its purity, but now the land would be cursed rather than blessed and would continually frustrate him. The final judgment pronounced—"till you return to the ground, for out of it you were taken; for you are dust, and to dust you shall return" (3:19)—not only fulfills the threat of death (2:17) but also means that Adam will be unable to attain his original destiny. Adam was called to image God by working in this world and then enjoying blessed life in the world-to-come, but now instead he will return to the dust in death.

This is another crucial issue for understanding Christianity and culture. The first Adam would find that his commission in this world was impossible to fulfill and therefore that his final destiny was impossible to achieve. Paul comments that "all have sinned and fall short of the glory of God" (Rom. 3:23) and later proclaims that "the wages of sin is death" (6:23). Human cultural life did not come to an end with the fall, but now cultural endeavors are plagued with

---

[8]For further explanation and defense of this understanding of the serpent and Adam's responsibilities toward him, see Meredith G. Kline, *Kingdom Prologue: Genesis Foundations for a Covenantal Worldview* (Overland Park, KS: Two Age Press, 2000), 119–21.

sinful failure. The end result is not glory, but death and destruction. *Fallen human culture cannot attain the new creation.*

Scripture has much to say about human sinfulness. For one thing, human sin is entirely derived from the first Adam and his act of rebellion in the garden: "sin came into the world through one man . . ." (Rom. 5:12). Adam's disobedience is not only the cause of our sinful disposition but also of God's judgment against us: "one trespass led to condemnation for all men . . ." (5:18). From the first Adam, therefore, come both our condemnation and our sinful nature. Human depravity, furthermore, is holistic, deep-rooted, and relentless (see Gen. 6:5; 8:21; Ps. 51:5; Rom. 3:10–18). Sinful human beings continue to engage in cultural enterprises and to accomplish many humanly worthwhile things. But whatever value other people may ascribe to such works from an earthly perspective, none of them can earn God's final approval. Paul remarks, "The mind that is set on the flesh is hostile to God, for it does not submit to God's law; indeed, it cannot. Those who are in the flesh cannot please God" (Rom. 8:7–8).

Thus the first Adam failed in his original cultural mandate and now all of his descendants' cultural activities are pervasively corrupted. The result of Adam's sin was the sentence of death, which meant falling short of his original destiny: royal rest in the world-to-come. The pages of Scripture testify that Adam's descendants are condemned to share the same doom: "many died through one man's trespass . . ." (Rom. 5:15). In Scripture, "death" most often refers to bodily death, the separation of the soul from the body. Other times it refers to spiritual death, in the sense that no religious good remains living within us: "you were dead in the trespasses and sins in which you once walked . . ." (Eph. 2:1–2). But most strikingly Scripture speaks of death in eschatological terms, as a death in the world-to-come that corresponds, however ominously, to the life in the world-to-come originally held out to Adam. In the words of Revelation 20:6, this is the "second death." However much fallen human beings may strive to pick up the baton from Adam and pursue the tasks of culture with an eye to an eternal prize, the quest is futile.

They will end up not enthroned with God in glory but condemned with the serpent in the lake of fire (Rev. 20:10, 14–15).

Conclusion: A Ray of Hope

The story of human history told to this point is one of terrible tragedy. God created human beings with a high office, a noble calling, and a glorious destiny. Adam had a great cultural task set before him, which was to find focus in his working and guarding the garden of Eden. Because he bore the divine likeness, the outcome of his royal work in this world should have been a royal rest in the world-to-come. But his failure to complete this task plunged the human race into guilt, condemnation, and corruption. The fallen human race cannot undertake its cultural endeavors with a righteousness acceptable to God, it finds the natural world largely uncooperative and beyond its control, and it faces everlasting death as the only outcome of its work in this world.

But we need not end on a bitter note. In one sense Genesis 1–3 already tells half of the biblical story, but the second half of the story is so amazing that Scripture devotes the last 99 percent of its pages to telling it. In fact, God gives us a glimpse into the second half before Genesis 3 even finishes, for he tells the serpent that his apparent victory will end in total defeat: "I will put enmity between you and the woman, and between your offspring and her offspring; he shall bruise your head, and you shall bruise his heel" (3:15). The second half of the story may be long and complex in many ways, but its main point is simple: "For as in Adam all die, *so also in Christ shall all be made alive*" (1 Cor. 15:22). What the first Adam should have done—bring the human race to everlasting life in the world-to-come by perfectly obeying his cultural commission—the second and last Adam has accomplished. Christ has attained the original human destiny, and done so on behalf of those who trust in him.

Jesus Christ the Last Adam

Redemption and Consummation

THE PREVIOUS CHAPTER ended on a note of hope, despite the terrible devastation of the fall into sin. Even before he pronounces judgment on Adam and Eve, God proclaims to the serpent: "I will put enmity between you and the woman, and between your offspring and her offspring; he shall bruise your head, and you shall bruise his heel" (Gen. 3:15). Theologians sometimes refer to this verse as the *protevangelium*, the first announcement of the gospel. In light of Genesis 1–2, the way that the gospel is announced here is quite striking. The first Adam was commissioned to exercise dominion as a king (1:26–28) and to guard the holy garden of Eden as a priest (2:15), which means that when the serpent appeared, Adam should have asserted his authority, vanquished him, and protected the holy temple of Eden. Now God announces in Genesis 3:15 that what Adam failed to do would be accomplished by one of Eve's own offspring. This offspring would assert authority over the enemy and vanquish him, inflicting not a minor blow but a mortal wound to the head. So this is the original gospel message: a Son of Adam will do what Adam should have done in the first place. A second and last Adam is coming.

The rest of the Old Testament unfolds this theme until the New Testament proclaims that the second Adam, the Lord Jesus Christ, has arrived. In Romans 5:12–19 and 1 Corinthians 15 Paul explicitly points to these two Adams as the hinges upon which all of history turns, and he teaches that the *second Adam* is also the *last Adam*: "Thus it is written, 'The first man Adam became a living being'; the last Adam became a life-giving spirit" (1 Cor. 15:45). Before the second Adam no one accomplished the task of the first Adam, and after the second Adam no one needs to accomplish it. <u>The last Adam has completed it once and for all.</u> Christians will attain the original destiny of life in the world-to-come, but we do so not by picking up the task where Adam left off but by resting entirely on the work of Jesus Christ, the last Adam who accomplished the task perfectly.

How did Christ accomplish Adam's original task perfectly? Jesus did not personally fill the earth with his descendants or exercise dominion over all creatures in his human nature during his earthly ministry. But as considered in chapter 2, Adam was to have his *entire* obedience in the *entire* world determined through a *particular* test in a *particular* location. So it was for the last Adam. Like the first Adam, the Lord Jesus was confronted by the devil who tried to entice Christ to obey him, and King Jesus resisted the devil and conquered him (Matt. 4:1–11; Col. 2:15; Heb. 2:14). Like the first Adam, the Lord Jesus was called to priestly service, and Christ the Great High Priest purified God's holy dwelling and opened the way for human beings back into his presence (Heb. 9:11–28; 10:19–22). Like the first Adam, the Lord Jesus was to enter God's royal rest in the world-to-come upon finishing his work perfectly, and this is precisely what Christ did, entering into heaven itself, taking his seat at God's right hand, ministering in the heavenly tabernacle, and securing our place in the world-to-come (Heb. 1:3; 4:14–16; 7:23–28).

This is absolutely essential for issues of Christianity and culture! <u>If Christ is the *last Adam*, then we are not new Adams.</u> To understand our own cultural work as picking up and finishing Adam's original task is, however unwittingly, to compromise the sufficiency of Christ's work. Christ perfectly atoned for all our sins, and hence we have no sins left to atone personally. Likewise, Christ perfectly sustained a time of testing similar to Adam's: he achieved the new creation through his flawless obedience in this world. He has left nothing yet to be accomplished. God indeed calls Christians to suffer and to pursue cultural tasks obediently through our lives. But to think that our sufferings contribute to atoning for sin or that our cultural obedience contributes to building the new creation is to compromise the all-sufficient work of Christ.

In this chapter I first describe the work of Jesus Christ the last Adam in his first coming: his life, death, resurrection, and ascension. In these great events Christ accomplished the task given to the first Adam (vanquishing Satan as a righteous priest and king in this world) and then attained the destiny held out to the first Adam (entering the glory of the world-to-come). Next I discuss the benefits that come to God's people by faith in Christ. Through Christ's work God not only forgives the sins of believers but also reckons them as those who have perfectly completed the first Adam's task. They are united with Christ, claim his victory as their own, and become citizens of heaven, the world-to-come. Believers are not returned to the position of the first Adam, called to win the world-to-come by their faithful cultural activities. Instead, God first grants them all the rights of the world-to-come as an accomplished fact and then calls them to cultural labor in this world as a grateful response. Finally, I consider the conclusion of the biblical story: the second coming of Christ. In this climactic event Christ will bring the present world and all of its cultural activities to a sudden and decisive end. Yet even as he sends the fire of judgment upon this world, he will call the new heaven and new earth, the New Jerusalem, "down out of heaven" (Rev. 21:1–2), and his people will become more than just citizens of the world-to-come—they will become residents too.

Christ's Life, Death, Resurrection, and Ascension: Completing the First Adam's Work, Attaining the First Adam's Destiny

The previous chapter introduced some important biblical teaching about the first Adam from Romans, 1 Corinthians, and Hebrews, and I now turn back to these books to explore what they say about

51

Christ as the last Adam. In short, they teach that by his life, death, resurrection, and ascension, the Lord Jesus Christ, as the second and last Adam, has completed the work of the first Adam and attained his original destiny.

Romans

In Romans 5:12–19 Paul identifies the first Adam as the cause of the sin, condemnation, and death that fill the world. He uses a variety of expressions to describe what Adam did: "one man's trespass" (5:15, 17), "one man's sin" (5:16), "one trespass" (5:18), and "one man's disobedience" (5:19). These expressions point to the fundamental truth that *one* person, acting at *one* particular point in history, plunged the human race into its misery. Yet Paul's purpose here is not to leave us in despair but to hold up the work of Christ. *One* person, acting at *one* particular point in history, did just the opposite of what Adam did. In contrast to the "one trespass" of Adam, Christ performed "one act of righteousness" (5:18). In contrast to "one man's disobedience," Christ provided "one man's obedience" (5:19). Christ obeyed his Father throughout his entire life, and that obedience culminated in his crucifixion.[1] Paul says elsewhere: "being found in human form, he humbled himself by becoming obedient to the point of death, even death on a cross" (Phil. 2:8). Do we want to understand the work of Christ? Paul instructs us to learn from Adam. As Adam represented his descendants and brought them death and condemnation, so Christ represented his people and brought life and justification. What Adam was supposed to do (obey and attain eternal life), Christ has done. Christ was perfectly obedient on behalf of his people.

1 Corinthians

While Romans 5:12–19 emphasizes how Christ is the last Adam insofar as he obeyed God with perfect righteousness, 1 Corinthians

---

[1]For further discussion of Romans 5:18–19 and an explanation of why Paul refers to Christ's entire life of obedience here, see e.g., David VanDrunen, "To Obey Is Better Than Sacrifice: A Defense of the Active Obedience of Christ in the Light of Recent Criticism," in *By Faith Alone: Answering the Challenges to the Doctrine of Justification*, ed. Gary L. W. Johnson and Guy P. Waters (Wheaton: Crossway, 2006), 139–46.

15 emphasizes how Christ is the last Adam insofar as he attained the original destiny held out to the first Adam. The goal of Adam's original cultural commission has been achieved! Paul's two references to Christ as the last Adam in 1 Corinthians (15:21–22, 45) are part of a lengthy explanation of the doctrine of the resurrection of the dead.

Paul explains that "in fact Christ has been raised from the dead, the firstfruits of those who have fallen asleep" (15:20). The Lord Jesus was the first person in all of history to be resurrected. Paul then immediately compares the two Adams: "For as by a man came death, by a man has come also the resurrection of the dead" (15:21). Adam failed in his task and died, but Christ, the last Adam, has gone where no person ever has, to *bodily* life beyond the grave. In his resurrection life "he must reign until he has put all his enemies under his feet" (15:25). Christ as the last Adam is reigning even now as the resurrected man. The first Adam was originally destined to rule the world-to-come (Heb. 2:5–8). He was to image God by completing his royal work on earth and then being enthroned with God in the glory of the seventh day. Paul proclaims that now Christ is enthroned in glory and hence is reigning as a king. Christ has attained Adam's destiny, and one day the defeat of all his enemies will be made manifest (15:26–28, 54–57). The first Adam brought death, but the last Adam has defeated death and attained the life of the world-to-come.

Later in 1 Corinthians 15 Paul responds to two questions: "How are the dead raised? With what kind of body do they come" (15:35)? First he explains that as different kinds of creatures in this world have different kinds of bodies (15:36–41), "so is it with the resurrection of the dead" (15:42). Our present bodies are perishable, dishonorable, and weak, but the resurrection body will be imperishable, honorable, and powerful (15:42–43). The chief contrast is that the present body is "natural" and the resurrection body "spiritual" (15:44–46). Paul is not saying that our present bodies are material while our resurrection bodies will be immaterial. Both now and at the resurrection we will truly have physical bodies. The difference between these bodies, Paul explains, is that our present bodies are earthly while our resurrection bodies will be heavenly. It all revolves around the two Adams: "The first man was from the earth, a man of dust; the second man is from heaven" (15:47). Thus what Paul means by a "natural" body is a body that comes from this world and is fit for this world, and what he means by a "spiritual" body is a body that comes from the world-to-come and is fit for the world-to-come— it is "spiritual" because it was resurrected by the Holy Spirit who comes from heaven (see Rom. 1:4; 8:11). This is so important because "flesh and blood cannot inherit the kingdom of God, nor does the perishable inherit the imperishable" (1 Cor. 15:50).[2]

In other words, no one can enter into the world-to-come with a body like the first Adam's. Christ the last Adam, resurrected with a heavenly, Spiritual body, has entered into that imperishable kingdom that the first Adam failed to attain. It is there that he now reigns.

Hebrews

Paul's teaching about the last Adam is echoed in Hebrews. In the previous chapter I discussed what Hebrews teaches about creation and fall. Even from the beginning the human race was destined to rule the world-to-come, but the fall means that we now do not see anything remotely resembling this high human destiny (2:5–8). But there is good news: though now we do not "see everything in subjection to him [the human race]" (2:8), "we see . . . Jesus" (2:9). When we look at the first Adam, we see only failure, but when we look at Jesus, the last Adam, we see faithful obedience and the attainment of the first Adam's goal.

Hebrews 2:9 encapsulates this truth: "But we see him who for a little while was made lower than the angels, namely Jesus, crowned with glory and honor because of the suffering of death, so that by the grace of God he might taste death for everyone." This short statement expresses four key thoughts. First, Jesus became lower than the angels for a little while; that is, through his incarnation he stepped into the first Adam's position (see 2:6–8). Second, he suffered death; as the rest of Hebrews elaborates, Jesus remained

---

[2]For helpful exegetical discussion of these issues in 1 Corinthians 15, see also Geerhardus Vos, *The Pauline Eschatology* (Grand Rapids: Eerdmans, 1972), 166–70.

perfectly obedient through a lifetime of suffering that ended with the cross. Third, he is now crowned with glory and honor because he suffered death; in other words, as a faithful priest he has attained the first Adam's destiny in the world-to-come. Finally, he has done all of this on behalf of others. We will return to this last theme shortly, but let us now consider a little more what Hebrews teaches about the first three themes.

Hebrews emphasizes that Christ has followed the exact pattern intended for the first Adam. He finished his work in this world perfectly and then entered into the glory of heaven where he now reigns. After calling the Son "the radiance of the glory of God and the exact imprint of his nature" (he is an even more precise image of God than the first Adam), the author states: "After making purification for sins, he sat down at the right hand of the Majesty on high, having become as much superior to angels as the name he has inherited is more excellent than theirs" (1:3–4). In Hebrews, the idea of "sitting down" indicates that his work in this world was truly *finished*—he did it perfectly and there is nothing left to accomplish. As God finished his work and then rested in Genesis 1–2, so the last Adam finished his work and then sat down, at God's own right hand, ruling even the angels.

All of these themes recur throughout Hebrews (in addition to what we already observed in 2:9). Unlike the first Adam, who failed to finish the task he began, Jesus completed his work perfectly, being "without sin" (4:15). In contrast to the first Adam, he conquered Satan (2:14). Through this work he became qualified as a perfect high priest "after the order of Melchizedek" (5: 10; see 7:1–28). The first Adam was to exercise dominion as a king (Gen. 1:26–28) and guard the garden as a royal priest (Gen. 2:15), thus Jesus became the perfect Priest-King, like Melchizedek who was "king of Salem, priest of the Most High God" (Heb. 7:1). Whereas the first Adam allowed God's original temple to be polluted and caused human beings to be expelled from his presence, Jesus has cleansed the holy place and won our re-entry into God's presence—not simply in an earthly sanctuary but in a heavenly sanctuary (9:11–28). Jesus achieved the original human destiny, "the world to come" (2:5). He "entered God's rest" when he "passed through the heavens" (4:10, 14), so that he is now "exalted above the heavens" (7:26) and "seated at the right hand of the throne of the Majesty in heaven, a minister in the holy places, in the true tent that the Lord set up . . ." (8:1–2). Having finished his work in this world, he "sat down at the right hand of God" (10:12). The great Priest and King has entered the world-to-come.

The Benefits of Christ's Work for His People: Sharing in the World-to-Come

Romans, 1 Corinthians, and Hebrews also contain some important themes that I did not mention in the previous section. These books teach not only about Christ and his work but also about the wonderful *benefits* of this work *for us*. It is now time to consider specifically what the work of Christ as the last Adam means for those who have faith in him. This has profound implications for the Christian's cultural activities in this world.

Romans, 1 Corinthians, and Hebrews teach that Christ has perfectly completed Adam's work, and thus God treats believers as though they themselves had perfectly completed Adam's work. Our sins are forgiven and we are declared righteous and obedient in God's sight—in other words, we have been *justified*. What is more, because Christ attained the destiny of Adam, believers now claim the rights, privileges, and responsibilities of the world-to-come. Because Christ "died and was raised," and lives no longer in the "flesh" of this world, "if anyone is in Christ, he is a new creation" (2 Cor. 5:15–17). Though we still live in this world, with all of its limitations, temptations, and hardships, our true identity even now is as citizens of a heavenly kingdom where Christ sits exalted. We have free access to that world-to-come through prayer and worship, and we should live as those who belong to it. Thus the Christian life should *not* follow the pattern that the first Adam was supposed to follow. Christians are not to pursue righteous obedience in this world and then, as a consequence, enter the world-to-come. Instead, Christians have been made citizens of the world-to-come by a free gift of grace and now, as a consequence, are to live righteous and obedient lives in this world. Christians do not pick up and continue the task of Adam. Thanks to the finished work of Christ, Christians should view their cultural activities in a radically different way from the way that the first Adam viewed his. We pursue cultural activities in response to the fact that the new creation has already been achieved, not in order to contribute to its achievement.

Romans

As noted, Christ offered "righteousness" and "obedience" to his Father, in contrast to the "trespass" and "disobedience" of Adam (Rom. 5:18–19). What is Paul's larger point in making this crucial claim? From Romans 1:18 all the way through the end of chapter 5 Paul's primary purpose is to explain the doctrine of *justification.* He begins by explaining that though God in his justice continues to require obedience to his law as a prerequisite for justification (that is, for being declared righteous in his sight) (2:13), human sin has totally disqualified us and made all people unable to be justified by their own obedience (1:18–3:20). But beginning in 3:21 Paul provides the answer to this terrible human predicament. Through the work of Christ God does two great things for the person who believes in him: he "counts righteousness apart from works" and he does "not count his sin" (4:6–8). The reason why God does not count the believer's sin against him is because God has put Christ Jesus "forward as a propitiation by his blood" (3:25). And the reason why God counts righteousness to the believer is because of Christ's "one act of righteousness," "the one man's obedience" (5:18–19). It is this righteousness that "leads to justification and life" (5:18). This is entirely a "free gift" of God (5:15–16), coming to the person who "does not work but believes in him who justifies the ungodly" (4:5). Because Christ has already perfectly completed the work that God requires of human beings in this world, people today need not add any of their own works to satisfy God—they need only rest in Christ who has done it all for them.[3]

God therefore does not call us back to complete the task that the first Adam fumbled. This is a key reason why I stated above that a

---

[3]For a detailed defense of the doctrine of justification very briefly summarized here, see J. V. Fesko, *Justification: Understanding the Classic Reformed Doctrine* (Phillipsburg, NJ: P&R, 2008). ✦

Protestant doctrine of justification is ultimately incompatible with a redemptive transformationist view of culture along the lines of neo-Calvinism, the New Perspective on Paul, or the emergent church. Our cultural task as already-justified Christians is fundamentally different from that of the first Adam, who was to perform his cultural work during a period of probation.

Paul also states that believers will "reign in life" (5:17). Thus believers are not only justified in Christ, but they will also share in his resurrection life and royal reign. Christ has been resurrected, so believers will be resurrected (8:11); Christ has been glorified, so believers will be glorified (8:17); Christ is reigning in glory, so believers will reign with him (2 Tim. 2:12). The two Adams theme in Romans is profoundly powerful. Because Christ was perfectly obedient where the first Adam failed, believers are reckoned as having been perfectly obedient (justification) and are assured that they will share in the resurrection life, glory, and reign of the last Adam (glorification).

1 Corinthians

1 Corinthians 15 elaborates on one of the truths taught in Romans: believers will share the resurrection life and royal reign in the world-to-come that Christ has attained. Paul uses the two Adams theme in 1 Corinthians 15 to explain the resurrection (15:12). He asserts that "Christ has been raised from the dead" and that he was raised as the "firstfruits of those who have fallen asleep" (15:20). This idea of *firstfruits* means that Christ is but the first of many who will be resurrected: "Christ the firstfruits, then at his coming those who belong to Christ" (15:23). Later Paul explains that the resurrected bodies of believers will be exactly the same kind of body as Christ himself already bears. "As was the man of dust, so also are those who are of the dust, and as is the man of heaven, so also are those who are of heaven. Just as we have borne the image of the man of dust, we shall also bear the image of the man of heaven" (15:48–49). We have borne the image of the first Adam in this life, and our bodies resemble Adam's body. But due to Christ's life, death, resurrection, and ascension we are destined to bear *Christ's* image. The first

Adam bore God's image insofar as he was called to work—toward the goal of royal life and rest if he succeeded. The last Adam bears God's image insofar as he has already succeeded in the work and has already attained the royal life and rest. Again we see that Christ does not restore us to Adam's original task but takes us to where Adam was supposed to arrive.

In his resurrection Christ was not resuscitated to life in this world but raised up to life in the world-to-come: "flesh and blood cannot inherit the kingdom of God, nor does the perishable inherit the imperishable" (15:50). This benefit of being resurrected with a new kind of body, fit not for this world but for the world-to-come, belongs to us as well as to Christ. "We shall all be changed, in a moment, in the twinkling of an eye, at the last trumpet," and "we shall be changed" (15:51–52). We shall never again die, for death will be completely defeated (15:53–55).

Hebrews

While saying little about the future resurrection of the body, Hebrews emphasizes believers' *present* access to the world-to-come. Though still dwelling in this world and having bodies like the first Adam's, they have the rights and privileges of the world-to-come, where Christ has gone before them.

According to Hebrews, not only has Jesus attained the original destiny of Adam, but we also are destined to follow where he has gone. Hebrews 2:9–10 speaks of Jesus, the one crowned with "glory and honor," as "bringing many sons to glory." Jesus is the "founder of their salvation"—"founder" being a Greek word that indicates a "pioneer" or "forerunner" (2:10). Jesus leads his children to "glory" in his wake. Likewise, because Jesus has "passed through the heavens" (4:14) "there remains a Sabbath rest for the people of God" (4:9).

Until the day we enter that rest with resurrected bodies, Jesus is there ministering for our sakes as the great and perfect high priest. He is "merciful and faithful . . . , able to help those who are being tempted" because "he himself suffered when tempted" (2:17–18). He is not "unable to sympathize with our weaknesses" because he "in every respect has been tempted as we are . . ." (4:15). As a priest "he always lives to make intercession for them" (7:25). Jesus is a priest "after the order of Melchizedek" (6: 20; see 7:1–28). The Old Testament priests ministered in a tabernacle that was "earthly" (9:1) and of "the present age" (9:9)—but Jesus, who has been "crowned with glory and honor" (2:9) and has "passed through the heavens" (4:14), now ministers in a different location. Jesus exercises his priesthood in a tabernacle "not made with hands, that is, not of this creation" (9:11), not in "holy places made with hands" but in "heaven itself" (9:24). And the reason why Jesus has gone into "heaven itself" is "to appear in the presence of God on our behalf" (9:24).

Since Christ is there before us, ministering on our behalf, Hebrews exhorts us "to draw near," and to do so with "confidence" and "full assurance of faith" (4:16; 10:22; see vv. 19–22). These invitations do not refer to a literalistic, bodily entrance into the world-to-come at the present time, but to a drawing near in prayer (4:16) and corporate worship (10:24–25). Our worship ultimately does not concern things that "may be touched" (12:18), for in worship we come "to Mount Zion and to the city of the living God, the heavenly Jerusalem, and to innumerable angels in festal gathering, and to the assembly of the firstborn who are enrolled in heaven, and to God, the judge of all, and to the spirits of the righteous made perfect, and to Jesus . . ." (12:22–24). No wonder that we should offer our worship "with reverence and awe" (12:28).

Thus Hebrews expresses in beautiful terms that while we still live in this world, we have a personal and intimate share in the life of the world-to-come, precisely because Jesus our forerunner has already entered it. For this reason, "here we have no lasting city, but we seek the city that is to come" (13:14). That city, "the city of the living God, the heavenly Jerusalem" (12:22), is the place where we already belong in a wonderful foretaste of the things to come, thanks not to our own works but to Christ's alone.

Citizenship in Heaven

Hebrews reminds us, therefore, that our true identity as believers in Christ is not defined by the things of this world but of the world-to-come. Paul makes this point by saying that our *life* and *citizenship* are in heaven.

Paul states, for example: "If then you have been raised with Christ, seek the things that are above, where Christ is, seated at the right hand of God. Set your minds on things that are above, not on things that are on earth. For you have died, and your life is hidden with Christ in God. When Christ who is your life appears, then you also will appear with him in glory" (Col. 3:1–4). Even in the present, Paul says, our true identity is in the world-to-come, the "things that are above." Our identity in this world, concerning "things that are on earth," does not truly define us. Christians ought to conduct themselves accordingly: "Put to death, therefore, what is earthly in you . . ." (3:5; see 3:5–4:6). Paul first tells them that they belong to the world-to-come, *then* he tells them how to live here and now.

In Philippians 3 Paul is again thinking about both the resurrection (3:10–11, 21) and the life that we live in between Christ's resurrection and ours. As in Colossians 3:2, the enemies of Christ set their minds "on earthly things," but "our citizenship is in heaven, and from it we await a Savior, the Lord Jesus Christ" (Phil. 3:19–20). Christians may happen to live in any city in this world, but what really matters is their citizenship in the world-to-come and their hope that Christ will soon return from that place.

In order to sustain us in our heavenly identity as we endure the trials and temptations of this world, Christ blesses us with many gifts, most notably the Holy Spirit sent from heaven (John 16:7; Acts 2:33). This heavenly Spirit is a "seal" and a "guarantee of our inheritance until we acquire possession of it" (2 Cor. 1:22; Eph. 1:14; see Eph. 4:30). Just as believers receive citizenship in heaven in Christ and are then called to act righteously in this world, so believers receive the Spirit and are thus empowered to act in a God-pleasing way. They do not do good works and then receive the Spirit as a reward, but receive the Spirit and then bring forth his "fruits" (Gal. 5:22–25).

What is the main point of this chapter thus far? Because of the obedience of the last Adam, a human being has already attained the life of the world-to-come, and believers, united to Christ, already participate in its life and have a share in its rights and privileges, without any need to earn them by their own obedience. They live in this world not in order to gain the world-to-come, for they have gained the world-to-come by a free gift of grace and are now called to live godly lives as a consequence.

God still calls us to engage in cultural labors. He has not taken us out of this world but entrusts us with a range of responsibilities within it. Yet we are not called to engage in cultural labors in order to attain or to build the world-to-come, the new creation. As noted in the first chapter, many recent books on Christianity and culture suggest that redemption in Christ consists in the *restoration* of God's good creation. They do not mean that we are placed literally back into the garden of Eden to start from the beginning, but that we resume Adam's original task of working and developing the creation. This includes reforming the cultural development that has occurred until now and continuing that development toward the original eschatological goal.[4] But this is *not* the New Testament's teaching. The New Testament does speak about the completion of the first Adam's original task and the attainment of his goal, but it always attributes this work to Christ, the last Adam. We have not been given a plot of land as a holy temple to work and to guard; Christ has already purified a place for God to dwell with his people. We have not been commissioned to conquer the devil; Christ has already conquered him. Christ did not come to restore the original creation, but to win the new creation and to bestow its blessings upon his people apart from their own efforts.

Thus Christians' cultural endeavors should *not* be understood as getting back to Adam's original task. This claim should become increasingly clear as we consider the final topic in this chapter. The story of the last Adam finally comes to its climax at his second coming, when he returns to this world from his glorious reign in the world-to-come. On that day the world-to-come will be revealed to our eyes, and the cultural activities and products of this world will come to a sudden and drastic end.

---

[4]See the description in chapter 1 of several writers associated with neo-Calvinism, the New Perspective on Paul, and the emerging church.

The Second Coming of Christ: The End of This World, the Revelation of the World-To-Come

Through his life, death, resurrection, and ascension, the Lord Jesus Christ has fulfilled the original task of the first Adam and attained his original destiny. Because of this work his saints already enjoy rich blessings as they stand justified before God's throne and participate in the things of the world-to-come as citizens of heaven. But the saints have not yet reached the final destination. They long to be residents of the world-to-come and not simply citizens from afar. The last Adam will return to this world in order to gather his saints for residence in the world-to-come.

The New Testament looks forward to one awesome day at the end of history, the "day of the Lord," when Christ will return, all the dead will be raised, all people will stand before the final judgment, and the present world will give way to the new heaven and new earth. The New Testament speaks of these events as happening simultaneously (e.g., John 5:28–29; Rom. 8:18–24; 1 Cor. 15:22–24; 1 Thess. 4:13–5:3; 2 Thess. 1:4–10; 2 Pet. 3:3–15).[5] This biblical testimony about the last day makes great sense in light of things already considered in this chapter. Thanks to Christ's life, death, resurrection, and ascension believers have already passed through judgment with him (justification) and been made citizens of the world-to-come. They stand on the very brink of eternity. The only thing left for them to receive is entrance into Christ's presence in the world-to-come with resurrected bodies. They are waiting for nothing else and nothing less can satisfy them.[6]

---

[5]For discussion and defense of this claim, see Robert B. Strimple, "Amillennialism," in *Three Views on the Millennium and Beyond*, ed. Darrell L. Bock (Grand Rapids: Zondervan, 1999), 100–12; and Kim Riddlebarger, *A Case for Amillennialism: Understanding the End Times* (Grand Rapids: Baker, 2003), 130–45.

[6]As Geerhardus Vos put it nearly a hundred years ago, "Paul looks upon the present Christian state as half-eschatological, because it is a state in the Spirit, the enjoyment of the first-fruits of the Spirit, the full possession of the Spirit constituting the life of heaven. The point may be made that, thus considered, the present so directly leads up to, so thoroughly pre-fashions the eternal future as to leave no room for a third something that would separate the one from the other. No matter with what concrete elements or colors the conception of a millennial state may be filled out, to a mind thus nourished upon the first-fruits of eternal life it can, for the very reason that it must fall short of eternal life, have neither significance nor attraction." See "The Second Coming of Our Lord and the Millennium," in *Redemptive History and Biblical Interpretation: The*

There are obviously many interesting questions that arise with regard to the second coming of Christ, but for purposes of this book the main question is this: what happens to the things of this world and particularly to the products of our cultural activity, in light of the revelation of the world-to-come in the new heaven and new earth? The New Testament teaches that the natural order as it now exists will come to a radical end and that the products of human culture will perish along with the natural order. As we have seen, Christ has already entered into the world-to-come, and now he is making it ready for us to join him (John 14:3). On the last day, after "the first heaven and the first earth" have "passed away," we will see "a new heaven and a new earth" when "the holy city, new Jerusalem," comes "down out of heaven from God" (Rev. 21:1–2). The world-to-come will be revealed amidst the destruction of the present world.

The End of the Natural Order

First, then, what will happen to the present natural order—the land, seas, and skies, "seedtime and harvest, cold and heat, summer and winter, day and night" (Gen. 8:22)—when Christ returns? Second Peter 3 provides a detailed account of the fate of the natural order on the last day, and it describes the natural order as meeting a devastating end (see also Rev. 6:12–14). Peter warns about scoffers who will taunt Christians by saying, "Where is the promise of his coming? For ever since the fathers fell asleep, all things are continuing as they were from the beginning of creation" (3:4). These scoffers deny Christ's coming on the evidence that things in this world continue on as they always have. Christ's coming and the end of this present world are intimately connected. Thus Peter responds: "by the same word [as at creation] the heavens and earth that now exist are stored up for fire, being kept until the day of judgment and destruction of the ungodly" (3:7). The promise of fire sounds ominous, and this is exactly how Peter meant it to sound: "The day of the Lord will come like a thief, and then the heavens will pass away with a roar,

Shorter Writings of Geerhardus Vos, ed. Richard B. Gaffin Jr. (Phillipsburg, NJ: Presbyterian and Reformed, 1980), 422.

and the heavenly bodies will be burned up and dissolved, and the earth and the works that are done on it will be exposed" (3:10). On the day of God "the heavens will be set on fire and dissolved, and the heavenly bodies will melt as they burn" (3:12).

Peter answers our question about the fate of the present natural order: it will be burned up, melt, and dissolve. God promised to Noah after the flood that "seedtime and harvest, cold and heat, summer and winter, day and night, shall not cease." But God prefaced that promise with the words "*while earth remains*" (Gen. 8:22). Second Peter 3 announces the coming of the time when earth will remain no more and the regularities of nature will cease, being dissolved in the consuming fire of the last day.

Hebrews 12 presents a similar picture. After explaining that we participate in the life of the heavenly Jerusalem even now (12:22–24), the author of Hebrews warns his readers not to reject God's warning from heaven (12:25). Then, after quoting from Haggai 2:6—"Yet once more I will shake not only the earth but also the heavens" (12:26)—he describes the future of the natural order: "This phrase, 'Yet once more,' indicates the removal of things that are shaken—that is, things that have been made—in order that the things that cannot be shaken may remain. Therefore let us be grateful for receiving a kingdom that cannot be shaken . . ." (12:27–28). As Hebrews 1:10–12 already hinted, the kingdom represented by the heavenly Jerusalem will endure forever, but the created things of this world will not.

According to Paul, creation waits "with eager longing for the revealing of the sons of God" (Rom. 8:19) and "the creation itself will be set free from its bondage to corruption and obtain the freedom of the glory of the children of God" (8:21). To understand Paul's point, it is important to remember that *this present world was never meant to exist forever*. The first Adam was commissioned to finish his task in this world and then to rule in the world-to-come (Heb. 2:5). Thus when creation groans (Rom. 8:22) for something better, for "the glory" that is coming (8:18), creation is not seeking an improvement of its present existence but the attainment of its original destiny. It longs to give way before the new heaven and new earth spoken of in 2 Peter 3 and Revelation 21.

Romans 8:18–23, however, also suggests that there will be some continuity between this world and the world-to-come. Paul's reference to the resurrection, "the redemption of our bodies" (8:23), may be a helpful clue for understanding where to find the continuity between the present heaven and earth and the new heaven and new earth. Paul says that the resurrection of believers is the focal point of creation's longing (8:19, 21, 23). Though Scripture teaches the destruction of the natural order, it does not teach its annihilation. In fact, we know that the present world will not be annihilated because Scripture teaches that our earthly bodies will be transformed into resurrected bodies. It is precisely this—*the resurrection of believers' bodies*—that the created order is now longing for: "the creation waits with eager longing for the revealing of the sons of God" (8:19). Our earthly bodies are the only part of the present world that Scripture says will be transformed and taken up into the world-to-come. *Believers themselves* are the point of continuity between this creation and the new creation. The New Jerusalem is the bride of Christ (Rev. 21:2). Asserting that anything else in this world will be transformed and taken up into the world-to-come is speculation beyond Scripture.

As a side note, it is important to emphasize that this conclusion is not meant to question the goodness of what is physical and visible or to deny the physical and visible character of the new creation. If there is a "problem" with the things of this present creation, it does not lie with the fact that they are physical and visible, but with the fact that they belong to a present creation that was never meant to be the final home of the human race (and with the fact that they have been corrupted by sin). The new creation will be physical and visible and inhabited by the resurrected bodies of the children of the last Adam.

The End of Present Human Culture

If the present natural order is destined for radical dissolution, then what does that mean for present human culture? Will the products of human culture—or at least the good ones, or the ones produced by Christians—somehow survive the consuming fire of the last day and adorn the new creation? Will the worthy cultural artifacts produced by Christians serve as "the building materials for that new earth?"[7] As we will consider in subsequent chapters, Scripture treats our cultural labors as meaningful and honorable, but this does not mean that they are meant to last forever. The New Testament teaches that the entirety of present cultural activities and products will be brought to a radical end, along with the natural order, at the second coming of Christ.

Second Peter 3 not only provides the most detailed description of what will happen to the natural order at Christ's second coming but it also mentions what will happen to this world's cultural products. The short answer is that 2 Peter 3 assigns the same fate to the products of human culture that it assigns to the natural order itself. Peter states: "The day of the Lord will come like a thief, and then the heavens will pass away with a roar, and the heavenly bodies will be burned up and dissolved, and the earth *and the works that are done on it* will be exposed" (3:10). Peter says, in essence, that the consuming fire of the last day will penetrate both God's handiwork and human handiwork.

Paul, the Gospels, and Revelation also teach that our present cultural activities and products will come to a radical end on the day of Christ's return. Paul states, for example: "The appointed time has grown very short. From now on, let those who have wives live as though they had none, and those who mourn as though they were not mourning, and those who rejoice as though they were not rejoicing, and those who buy as though they had no goods, and those who deal with the world as though they had no dealings with it. For the present form of this world is passing away" (1 Cor. 7:29–31). Paul assumes that his Christian readers will be engaged in the affairs of human culture. They will marry, they will buy and sell, they will have dealings with the world, and they will mourn and rejoice because of earthly events. But they will not be overwhelmed by these things or treat them as if they were of ultimate importance. This is because the world in its present form is passing away. Even important and

---

[7]Anthony A. Hoekema, *The Bible and the Future* (Grand Rapids: Eerdmans, 1979), 287.

worthy things such as marriage and commercial activity will meet the same fate as the natural order. Marriage, commerce, and the products of culture can be very good things, but they are temporary. In 1 Corinthians, Paul speaks only of the ministry of the church, not general cultural activity, as that which is, in some sense, permanent (3:12–15; 15:58).[8] Elsewhere Paul writes: "we look not to the things that are seen but to the things that are unseen. For the things that are seen are transient, but the things that are unseen are eternal" (2 Cor. 4:18). In 1 Timothy 6:7 he adds, echoing Ecclesiastes 5:15: "We brought nothing into the world, and we cannot take anything out of the world."

Christ communicated a similar message: "As were the days of Noah, so will be the coming of the Son of Man. For as in those days before the flood they were eating and drinking, marrying and giving in marriage, until the day when Noah entered the ark, and they were unaware until the flood came and swept them all away, so will be the coming of the Son of Man" (Matt. 24:37–39). God informed Noah of his intention to destroy both "all flesh" and "the earth" (Gen. 6:13), and the flood brought all cultural activities to a sudden end. It wiped out all products of human culture, except the ark, which served as a means of saving Noah's family and a pair of every kind of animal (Genesis 7). As a foretaste of the last day, therefore, the flood indicates that the products of present human culture are doomed to destruction with the natural order itself.

Finally, Revelation 18 presents a startling picture of the destiny of present human culture when it tells of the fall of Babylon. Babylon is a complex image in Revelation, indicating the societies of this world in which the false church and the world's political powers

---

[8] In 1 Corinthians 3:14 Paul speaks of "work" that will "survive" on the last day. In the context of 1 Corinthians 1–3, however, it is specifically the work of ministering the gospel and building the church that Paul has in mind. This has nothing to do with well-composed pieces of music or well-constructed houses surviving into the new creation. First Corinthians 15:58 is similar. There Paul encourages his readers to know "that in the Lord your labor is not in vain." What does he have in mind? In the previous verses he has instructed them about the resurrection of their bodies for life in the coming kingdom of God, not about the survival of any of their cultural products for existence in the world-to-come. And in the following verses (i.e., 1 Corinthians 16), Paul speaks only about the life of the church, and nothing about general cultural activity.

exist in uneasy alliance.[9] One of the striking features of "Babylon" in Revelation 18 is that it is a place humming with cultural activity. It is the place of "kings" and "merchants" (18:3). It is the marketplace for "cargo of gold, silver, jewels, pearls, fine linen, purple cloth, silk, scarlet cloth, all kinds of scented wood, all kinds of articles of ivory, all kinds of articles of costly wood, bronze, iron and marble, cinnamon, spice, incense, myrrh, frankincense, wine, oil, fine flour, wheat, cattle and sheep, horses and chariots, and slaves . . ." (18:12–13). It is a purveyor of the arts—"of harpists and musicians, of flute players and trumpeters" (18:22). It is the worksite for the "craftsman" and the "mill" (18:22). It is where "bridegroom and bride" establish new families (18:23). Politics, commerce, music, and family all contribute to the life of Babylon. Revelation 18, however, describes the fall of this cosmopolitan commercial center. When the seventh bowl is poured out at the end of history, "God remembered Babylon the great, to make her drain the cup of the wine of the fury of his wrath" (16:19). And thus an angel from heaven announces, "Fallen, fallen is Babylon the great . . ." (18:2)! This means that her commerce, music, labor, and marriage can be found no more (18:11, 21–23).

It is important to note that *Christians* presently participate in the cultural activities of Babylon. As explained in later chapters, Christians today engage in the same politics, the same commerce, the same music, and the same institution of marriage that nonbelievers do. Though Christians are called to pursue these activities with righteousness and suffer persecution at the hands of Babylon, Christians and non-Christians share many cultural endeavors in common. Christians are not summoned to withdraw into their own cultural ghettos, but their cultural activities are intertwined with those of the world at large. As God required the Israelites of old to engage in normal cultural activities as exiles in the historic city of

---

[9]The identification of Babylon in Revelation is a disputed matter. For defense of the idea that Babylon is not Rome (or any other *particular* city), though John's readers may have seen characteristics of Babylon when they looked at Rome, see e.g., Iain Provan, "Foul Spirits, Fornication and Finance: Revelation 18 from an Old Testament Perspective," *Journal for the Study of the New Testament* 64 (1996): 81–100. For a detailed exposition of Revelation along the lines of how I understand its basic message, see e.g., Dennis E. Johnson, *Triumph of the Lamb: A Commentary on Revelation* (Phillipsburg, NJ: P&R, 2001).

Babylon (Jer. 29:4–9), so he expects Christians today to engage in normal cultural activities as residents of "Babylon," the social and economic institutions of our own time. And like the Israelites who left their houses and gardens behind in Babylon to return to Jerusalem (Jer. 29:10–14), so believers today await the time when they will see destroyed the activities and products of human culture—to which they themselves contributed—and they are welcomed into "the new Jerusalem, coming down out of heaven" (Rev. 21:2).

In his description of the New Jerusalem in Revelation 21, John remarks that by the light of the Lamb "the nations walk, and the kings of the earth will bring their glory into it. . . . They will bring into it the glory and the honor of the nations" (21:24, 26). Some writers use this statement as evidence that worthy cultural products of the nations of this world will be preserved to adorn the new creation.[10] Is this true, despite what we have seen in so many other places in Scripture? Should Christians expect to see the best of their cultural labors in the New Jerusalem? There is no reason to read Revelation 21:24–26 in a way that is inconsistent with the rest of the New Testament. In the context of Revelation (and of Isaiah 60, to which Revelation 21:24–26 alludes), the "nations" and "kings" refer to *Christians*, and the "honor" and "glory" that they bring in are their worship and praise.[11] In the new heaven and new earth, God's people, *in contrast to their prior experience*, will have houses and fields that endure, "and the former things shall not be remembered

---

[10]E.g., see Hoekema, *The Bible and the Future*, 285–86.

[11]In Isaiah 60 the nations will come to Jerusalem as part of the promise of the gospel going through the world and the Gentile peoples turning to God. In Revelation, the kings of the earth often refer to the ungodly rulers of this world, but in several places God's people are described in kingly fashion (e.g., 3:12; 5:9; 20:4). No one but believers are allowed into the New Jerusalem (21:27; 22:14–15), and the ungodly rulers of this world have been destroyed in the judgment upon Babylon (18:3), and thus the nations and kings of Revelation 21 must be Christians. Furthermore, John speaks of the kings and nations bringing their "glory and honor" into the new creation, not their "wealth," of which Isaiah 60:5 speaks. John seems purposefully to change the reference from material possessions to worship, for to give glory to God throughout Revelation is an act of worship (e.g., 15:4; 19:1). Revelation 21:24–26, therefore, refers not to earthly kings and nations bringing cultural products into the world-to-come but to Christians offering praise to their Savior. My thanks to the Rev. Zach Keele for his fine sermon on this text at Escondido Orthodox Presbyterian Church in January 2009 and for giving me a copy of his manuscript.

or come into mind" (Isa. 65:17; see vv. 17–25). Unlike the cultures of this world, the things of the world-to-come will last forever.

Conclusion

In this chapter I have concluded the tale of the two Adams. The last Adam has completed the task of the first Adam in this world, has attained his original destiny of life in the world-to-come, has given to his people a share in that world-to-come even now, and is coming again to bring the present world to a drastic conclusion and to reveal the new heavens and new earth to his waiting people. Therefore Christians are not called to pursue cultural activities as a way of attaining the world-to-come, nor should they expect the products of their cultural labors to survive into the new creation.

Why, then, do Christians work, study, and vote? What place does human culture have in this transient and passing world? To answer these questions part 2 considers what Scripture says about the cultural life of God's people between the fall and the second coming of Christ. We will see the importance of the two kingdoms for understanding the nature of the Christian's cultural work in this world. That work is honorable activity even though it does not build the new heaven and new earth.

PART TWO

LIVING IN BABYLON

Christians stand on the very brink of eternity. Jesus Christ, the last Adam, has completed the work of the first Adam and entered the new creation. Because Christ did this for us, we now belong to him and share in the rights and privileges of the world-to-come. We have been "justified by his grace as a gift" (Rom. 3:24) and made "fellow heirs with Christ" so that "we may also be glorified with him" (Rom. 8:17). We have been "raised with Christ" (Col. 3:1) and thus our "life is hidden with Christ in God" (Col. 3:3) and our "citizenship is in heaven" (Phil. 3:20). Because Jesus has "passed through the heavens," we today may "with confidence draw near to the throne of grace" (Heb. 4:14, 16), having "confidence to enter the holy places" (Heb. 10:19). We eagerly await Christ's return from heaven when he will "transform our lowly body to be like his glorious body" (Phil. 3:21) and we will see "a new heaven and a new earth . . . , the holy city, new Jerusalem, coming down out of heaven from God . . ." (Rev. 21:1–2). In light of these things, God has called us "to wait for his Son from heaven . . ." (1 Thess. 1:10).

The Christian life is one of waiting, but what is our identity in this world while we wait? We are citizens of heaven, but how do we relate to earthly activities and institutions? Peter uses some very interesting terms that form a crucial part of the answer. Peter calls Christians "exiles" and "sojourners" who are in "dispersion," using the Greek term *diaspora* that refers to the scattering of Jews throughout the world after being expelled from the Promised Land (1 Pet. 1:1, 17; 2:11). What is Peter saying about our identity in this world? By using the terms "exile" and "dispersion" Peter informs Christians that their identity is similar to that of the Old Testament Israelites who were driven from their land and lived far from home, many of them in Babylon. As we saw at the end of chapter 3, Revelation 18 refers to this present world, teeming with cultural activities, as "Babylon," and Christians are like exiles living in the midst of it. By using the term "sojourner" Peter points even further back in the Old Testament, to the days of Abraham, Isaac, and Jacob. As "sojourners" (Gen. 12:10; 15:13; 20:1; 21:34; 23:4), they were promised a land of their own but had not yet attained full possession of it. Like the patriarchs, Christians today are "in a foreign land" (Heb. 11:9; see 11:8–10, 13–16).

If we wish to understand the Christian's place in this world, therefore, we must go back to the Old Testament to learn about the themes of sojourning and exile and then, from the New Testament, inquire how we are sojourners and exiles today. In part 2 we will do exactly this. Chapter 4 begins in Genesis 3 immediately after the fall into sin and explores the relationship of God's people to the cultural life of this world in the Old Testament, with special attention to the experiences of Abraham and the exiles in Babylon. Then chapter 5 examines how the themes of sojourning and exile continue into the New Testament, and also how these themes change in some very important ways through the first coming of Christ, the proclamation of his kingdom, and the establishment of the church. In these chapters I will trace the emergence of the *two kingdoms* by which God rules this world. I will begin to explain why it is so helpful to understand these two kingdoms if we wish to be godly participants in civil society, to live in this world without being of this world (John 17:14–16), and to honor the idea that Christ, the last Adam, has already fulfilled the original commission given to Adam.

Old Testament Sojourners

IN HIS PROCLAMATION OF JUDGMENT in Genesis 3, God announces a coming Messiah who will crush the head of the serpent and bring about God's purposes for the world. God kept his promise by sending the Lord Jesus Christ, the last Adam, to live, die, rise, and ascend to heaven. But a very long time elapsed between the making of this promise and its fulfillment by Christ. In the meantime God dealt with the world in a variety of ways, preparing the way for Christ to come in "the fullness of time" (Gal. 4:4). That long and often complicated history is recorded in the Old Testament, and in telling this history the Old Testament has much to say that is crucial for understanding the nature and purpose of human culture and believers' relationship to it.

Chapter 4 explores this Old Testament teaching. We will see that God creates a deep and fundamental *spiritual antithesis* between believers and unbelievers and also that God ordains a broad *cultural commonality* that believers and unbelievers share. In describing these things I will identify the origin of the two kingdoms. To summarize, God founds the two kingdoms by means of two covenants. The covenant with Noah (Genesis 9) formally establishes and regulates the *common kingdom*. The covenant with Abraham (Genesis 15, 17) formally establishes and regulates the *redemptive* kingdom.[1] By observing the development of these two kingdoms in the Old Testament we can begin to understand what the New Testament means when it refers to Christians, living in this world and participating in human culture, as sojourners and exiles.

Spiritual Antithesis and Cultural Commonality

Genesis 4 records the early history of the human race after the fall into sin and relates many important things about the religious commitment of these early generations and the cultural life of humanity in its youth. We will see that though a person's religious commitments and his cultural life are interrelated, things often do not work out in the way we would expect. Believers and unbelievers are radically different from one another in very important ways, but they also share much in common in their cultural life in the present world, and unbelievers often surpass believers in cultural accomplishments. In order to appreciate what Genesis 4 says about these things it is helpful to go back briefly to the curses that God pronounces in Genesis 3:14–19.

Two fundamental truths taught in Genesis 3:14–19 are particularly relevant here: there will be a basic *spiritual antithesis* between believers and unbelievers in the subsequent history of the human race, but there will also be a great deal of *cultural commonality* among them. These two truths could easily be misunderstood, so a little explanation may be helpful. The idea of a spiritual antithesis appears clearly in God's words to the serpent in 3:15: "I will put enmity between you and the woman, and between your offspring and her offspring; he shall bruise your head, and you shall bruise his heel." When it comes to the essential and most important things in life, those allied with the woman and those allied with the serpent are enemies and hostile to one another. They believe in different

---

[1] I write "*formally* establishes and regulates" because the redemptive kingdom is already present in seed form in the promise of a coming Messiah in Genesis 3:15 and the common kingdom is already operative in the prophecies and events concerning human culture described in Genesis 3:16–19; 4:15–22, as this chapter will discuss. The covenants with Noah and Abraham formalize realities that had already been present in human history.

things, serve different masters, and are headed for different destinies (salvation or damnation). There is no middle ground and no zone of moral neutrality—each person belongs either to one master or the other. And whether a person belongs to Christ or belongs to Satan will have profound implications for how he thinks and acts in this world.

The idea of cultural commonality also appears in Genesis 3. We might expect, if the human race is fundamentally divided between the seed of the serpent and the seed of the woman, that nothing would be shared in common by all of humanity. Yet Genesis 3:16–19 indicates otherwise. All women—believers or unbelievers—will undergo pain when bearing children. All men—believers or unbelievers—will till the ground with hardship. All human beings—believers or unbelievers—will return to the dust. The human race as a whole will endure a common curse in this world: painful childbirth, backbreaking toil, and physical death. The human race as a whole will also enjoy common blessings in this world: childbirth, productive labor, and the continuation of life for a time. Thus Genesis 3:14–19 teaches both that a fundamental spiritual antithesis will divide believers from unbelievers and that a cultural commonality will result in many shared activities and experiences among them all.

Scripture immediately displays how this will work out in human history. The first part of Genesis 4 narrates the story of Cain and Abel. The spiritual antithesis is alive and well in this story, and it bears deadly fruit. Abel belongs to the offspring of the woman, and the Lord "had regard for Abel and his offering" (4:4), but Cain belongs to the offspring of the serpent, and "for Cain and his offering he [God] had no regard . . ." (4:5). Thus Cain lures Abel into the field, and he attacks and kills him (4:8). From the beginning the serpent brought death to the human race (3:19; John 8:44), and now the serpent's offspring promotes death on earth by slaying a believer in the true God. Cain becomes the prime biblical example of wickedness (see Heb.11:4; 1 John 3:12; Jude 11).

Yet immediately thereafter the story takes an interesting turn. God speaks with Cain and, as we might expect, pronounces judgment upon him, driving him away to be "a fugitive and a wanderer on the earth" (Gen. 4:12; see vv. 10–12). But when Cain protests that he cannot bear this curse and will be killed by anyone who finds him, God places a "mark" on Cain and swears an oath to him: "If anyone kills Cain, vengeance shall be taken on him sevenfold . . ." (4:15). God ordains that there will be justice in this world. "Sevenfold" justice indicates that this justice should be perfect and proportionate: punishments should fit the crimes. What is important to notice is that God promises justice and order in this world *to an unbeliever*. God indicates that there will be legal systems to curb the outbreak of evil, and even unbelievers will participate in them and benefit from them. So here is the first evidence of one important aspect of human cultural life: maintaining justice.

Three other important cultural activities are mentioned a few verses later. Jabal, Jubal, and Tubal-Cain become pioneers in three great areas of human culture: agriculture, music, and metallurgy. Jabal "was the father of those who dwell in tents and have livestock," Jubal "was the father of all those who play the lyre and pipe," and Tubal-cain "was the forger of all instruments of bronze and iron" (4:20–22). A striking fact grabs our attention. The people who make these great advances in human civilization do not belong to the godly line of Seth recorded in Genesis 5 but are descendants of the unbelieving Cain. Already at this early point in human history, as Genesis 3:16–19 anticipated, unbelievers as well as believers participate in cultural activities—and unbelievers may be higher achievers. Genesis 4 will not allow us to get overly optimistic about the cultural achievements of unbelievers, however, for it goes on to report that Lamech, father of the talented Jabal, Jubal, and Tubal-cain, was a murderer who scoffed at justice (4:23–24). Human history, it seems, will be a tale of great accomplishments combined with great evil. By God's will, cultural commonality will exist alongside the spiritual antithesis.

The Covenant with Noah and the Establishment of the Common Kingdom

Despite the cultural progress recorded in Genesis 4, evil gains the upper hand as history moves along. The population increases on earth (Gen. 6:1), but God sees how wicked the human race has become and resolves to "blot out man whom I have created from the face of the land . . ." (6:7; see vv. 5–7). God keeps his word and destroys the world with a great flood, wiping out people and animals alike. Even in this dark time of human history, however, God preserves a pious remnant: "Noah found favor in the eyes of the LORD" (6:8). Godly Noah stands in spiritual antithesis to the degenerate mass of humanity around him, and the Lord saves him, his family, and a pair of every kind of animal aboard the ark.

After the flood waters recede and they disembark, a very significant event sets the course for the subsequent history of human civilization: God enters into a covenant with Noah and every living creature. With this covenant the identity of one of the *two kingdoms* begins to come into focus. What I have called the "common kingdom" is formally established in the covenant that God makes with Noah in Genesis 8:20–9:17. By this covenant God ordains that there will be a stable natural order until the end of the world. All living creatures will live within this order, and the entire human race will engage in a variety of cultural activities. Several important features characterize this common kingdom established by the Noahic covenant: it concerns *ordinary cultural activities* (rather than special acts of worship or religious devotion), it embraces the human race *in common* (rather than a holy people that are distinguished from the rest of the human race), it ensures the *preservation* of the natural and social order (rather than the redemption of this order), and it is established *temporarily* (rather than permanently).

First, the common kingdom established by the Noahic covenant concerns *ordinary cultural activities*. God gives Noah (and his sons) several commands in 9:1–7 that illustrate this. God commands them to be "fruitful and multiply and fill the earth" (9:1; see v. 7) and gives them both plants and meat for eating (9:3–4). He also ordains that they should take judicial action against those who commit great wrongs such as murder: *by man* shall the murderer's blood be shed (9:5–6). These verses reflect the original cultural mandate given to Adam and Eve in Genesis 1:26–28, though with important differences. On the one hand, God repeats (twice) to Noah the original command to be fruitful and multiply and, echoing the original command to exercise dominion and to subdue the earth, he establishes human authority over the animals (9:2–4) and ordains judicial punishment of law-breakers (9:5–6). On the other hand, this covenant gives no commands about special acts of religious devotion, such as faith, prayer, or worship. The Noahic commands do not require people to function as priests. Furthermore, God never indicates that they can attain life in the world-to-come through obedience. Cultural responsibilities under Noah are therefore similar to, yet very different from, Adam's original cultural responsibilities.

2). Second, the kingdom established by the Noahic covenant embraces the human race *in common*. God makes no distinction among human beings but makes this covenant generally with "your offspring after you" for "all future generations" (9:9, 12). This covenant embraces not only all human beings but also "every living creature" (9:10, 12, 15, 16) and even the earth itself (9:13). Therefore this covenant does not identify a holy people of God distinguished from the rest of the human race.

3). Third, the common kingdom established by the Noahic covenant ensures the *preservation* of the natural and social order. God proclaims that "seedtime and harvest, cold and heat, summer and winter, day and night, shall not cease" (8:22). Wild animals will not overrun human civilization (9:2). Marriage and procreation will continue (9:1, 7). Social order will be protected by the administration of proportionate justice: "whoever sheds the blood of man, by man shall his blood be shed . . ." (9:6). But while this covenant promises the *preservation* of the natural and social order, it never promises its *redemption*. It delivers no assurance of salvation or the forgiveness of sins.[2] Even the covenant sign, the rainbow, is unlike the

---

[2] Two verses, Genesis 6:18 and 8:20, may raise questions about this statement. Genesis 6:18 speaks of a covenant that God makes with Noah, in which he promises him salvation from the flood by entering the ark. The evidence strongly points to the conclusion that this is a different covenant from the one mentioned in Genesis 9, however. God makes this first covenant only with Noah and his immediate family (not with every living creature), he makes different promises (of salvation from the flood rather than preservation of the world), and its terms are fulfilled by Genesis 8 (rather than being in effect until the end of the world). Genesis 8:20 records a sacrifice offered by Noah after he left the ark, immediately before God states that he will preserve the world. This sacrifice does not, however, mean that the Noahic covenant is redemptive rather than common.

signs of later biblical covenants (such as circumcision, the Passover, baptism, and the Lord's Supper): it does not symbolize the taking away of sins through the shedding of blood. It simply symbolizes the maintenance of this world (9:12–17).

Fourth, the common kingdom established by the Noahic covenant is put into place *temporarily*. To be sure, this covenant is going to last for a very long time, but it will come to an end at some point: "*While the earth remains*, seedtime and harvest, cold and heat, summer and winter, day and night, shall not cease" (8:22). God will not destroy the earth again *with a flood* (9:11, 15), but the present world will be terminated in some other way (by fire, at Christ's second coming, according to 2 Peter 3). From its outset, therefore, God ordained the common kingdom to serve temporary purposes until the return of Christ brings it to an end.

In summary, the Noahic covenant of Genesis 8:20–9:17 constitutes the formal establishment of the common kingdom. This means that *God himself established and rules the common kingdom*. It exists under the lordship of the triune God—Father, Son, and Holy Spirit. The common kingdom is not in any sense a realm of moral neutrality or human autonomy. During the early history recorded in Genesis 4 cultural commonality existed alongside a spiritual antithesis. God put an end to that cultural commonality when he separated Noah's family from the rest of the human race at the time of the flood, but after the flood he reestablished that cultural commonality by means of a covenant. For the rest of the history of this world God ordains that the cycles of nature will continue in regular patterns, and that all people—whether believer or unbeliever—should engage in ordinary cultural activities such as marrying and childbearing, eating and drinking, and enforcing justice against those who disrupt the social order. The Noahic covenant itself does not tell us about the spiritual antithesis between believers and unbelievers, but this theme soon emerges again as the story of the Old Testament continues to unfold.

For one thing, Noah offers this sacrifice *after* he has been saved by God from the destruction of the world, and it appears to be a sacrifice of consecration rather than of expiation for sins. God's covenant words in the following verses, furthermore, mention nothing about forgiveness or eternal salvation.

The Covenant with Abraham and the Establishment of the Redemptive Kingdom

Genesis 10–11 describes some of the people and events after the days of Noah when human beings again spread out and populated the earth. These chapters include the famous account of the Tower of Babel (11:1–9). This act of pride reminds readers that though God has ordained the common kingdom to be one in which believers and unbelievers together will pursue beneficial cultural activities, it is also a kingdom whose citizens are prone to wickedness and rebellion against God. The spiritual antithesis is at work within it. At Babel the spirit of the serpent asserts itself and turns the legitimate pursuit of human civilization into a self-glorifying act of defiance. But God's judgment against this project keeps the full outbreak of wickedness in check so that the life of the common kingdom—and human history generally—can continue. Believers in the true God should acknowledge and appreciate the God-ordained character of the common kingdom, but they must always be on guard against its tendency toward rebellion. It has both divine origins and demonic proclivities.

The end of Genesis 11 introduces us to one of the major figures of Scripture: Abram (later called Abraham). At first there seems to be nothing special about him. He lives in Ur of the Chaldeans and has a wife named Sarai, or Sarah. But soon God sets him apart from the rest of the human race and a new chapter in history begins. Whereas God made a covenant with Noah in Genesis 9 and thereby formally established the common kingdom, God makes a covenant with Abraham in Genesis 15 and 17 and thereby formally establishes the *redemptive kingdom*. Scripture portrays Abraham as living a two-kingdoms way of life.

In the previous section I identified four key features of the common kingdom, as revealed in the Noahic covenant. The Abrahamic covenant bears the opposite features: it concerns *religious faith and worship* (rather than ordinary cultural activities), it embraces a *holy people* that is *distinguished* from the rest of the human race (rather than the human race in common), it *bestows the benefits of salvation* upon this holy people (rather than preserving the natural and social order), and it is established *forever and ever* (rather than temporarily). This covenant makes the spiritual antithesis obvious. Here God sets apart a people who, because of their faith and obedience toward him, are radically distinguished from their neighbors and given a different eternal destiny (life with Christ in the world-to-come). Genesis teaches these things about the Abrahamic covenant.

First, several events in Abraham's life show that the redemptive kingdom is about *religious faith and worship* rather than about ordinary cultural activities. Just before he makes a covenant with Abraham (15:9–21), for example, God promises to make his descendants as numerous as the stars in the sky (15:5). In response, Abraham "believed the LORD, and he counted it to him as righteousness" (15:6). In the New Testament Paul would look back to this response as a prime example of saving faith (Rom. 4:1–25; Gal. 3:1–9). Faith is the most basic response to the promises of the covenant with Abraham, though faith should also produce good works as its fruit (see Genesis 22; James 2:14–26). Another example is when God renews his covenant with Abraham and instructs him and his descendants to "keep" it, through a religious rite or sacramental ritual: circumcising all of the males in his household (Gen. 17:9–14). Later Abraham is distinguished from the Philistines among whom he lived by the fact that he "called . . . on the name of the LORD, the Everlasting God" (21:33). In this covenant God gives Abraham no instructions about how to engage in ordinary cultural activities, but he turns him from worshiping idols to worshiping the one true God (see Josh. 24:2).

Second, through the Abrahamic covenant God establishes a redemptive kingdom that embraces a *holy people* who are *distinguished* from the rest of the human race. Unlike the covenant with Noah, God makes this covenant not with the whole of humanity and all living creatures but with "you [Abraham] and your offspring after you" (Gen. 17:7). This covenant does not unite the human race in a common experience and enterprise but separates and distinguishes a part of the human race from the rest of it, precisely through its religious faith and worship. Though this separated part of the human race was initially tiny (one household), God promised that a great multitude of people would participate in this wonderful covenant

83

(12:2; 15:5; 17:4–6). This covenant is not universal in the sense of encompassing every single individual, but it is universal in the sense that "all the families of the earth shall be blessed" through Abraham (12:3). Genesis leaves us wondering how exactly these great promises will be fulfilled, but the New Testament explains it: in the last days all people of faith are the children of Abraham (Gal. 3:7–9, 29). The covenant with Abraham has a universal dimension because in Christ "there is neither Jew nor Greek, there is neither slave nor free, there is no male and female . . ." (Gal. 3:28). A special people of God will be taken "from every tribe and language and people and nation," and God will make them "a kingdom" (Rev. 5:9–10).

Third, the covenant with Abraham formally establishes a kingdom that *bestows the benefits of salvation* upon this holy people set apart from the world. Unlike the Noahic covenant, this covenant is not about preserving this present world but about opening up the gates of the world-to-come. This is concisely illustrated in Abraham's response to God's promises in Genesis 15:6: "he believed the Lord, and he counted it to him as righteousness." According to Paul, this phrase refers to justification by faith. That is, God does not count Abraham's sin against him but credits to him the righteousness of another, namely, Christ (Rom. 4:1–8; 5:17–19). The justified person has "peace with God through our Lord Jesus Christ" and is "saved by him from the wrath of God" (Rom. 5:1, 9).

Fourth and finally, God establishes the covenant with Abraham not temporarily but as a kingdom meant to endure forever and ever. This point was implied in the previous paragraph, since the blessing of justification grants nothing less than eternal life. But this point is reinforced in Genesis 17:6, where God says to Abraham: "I will make you into nations, and kings shall come from you." As discussed in chapter 3, the place where we ultimately see nations and kings coming from Abraham is in the new heaven and new earth, the New Jerusalem: "The city has no need of sun or moon to shine on it, for the glory of God gives it light, and its lamp is the Lamb. By its light will the nations walk, and the kings of the earth will bring their glory into it" (Rev. 21:23–24). The "nations and kings" created by the covenant with Abraham are not the nations and kings that come and go in this world, but believers, who constitute the eternal redemptive kingdom that will rule the world-to-come with Christ, in glorious fulfillment of the original human destiny (Heb. 2:5–9). It is through the covenant with Abraham, therefore, that people come to belong to the Lord Jesus Christ as the last Adam, the seed of the woman, and have hope of joining him in the world-to-come.

These four features of the Abrahamic covenant indicate that it was meant to endure long beyond the days of Abraham himself. Theologians sometimes use the term "the covenant of grace" to describe the continuation, progress, and fulfillment of the Abrahamic covenant through the rest of history.[3] In the Mosaic covenant, the Davidic covenant, and the new covenant God remembers and fulfills his promises to Abraham in ever new ways, until the day when his saving purposes are brought to completion in the world-to-come, the new heaven and new earth. This is what I refer to by the term "covenant of grace" in subsequent pages. The rest of chapter 4 and chapter 5 will trace the progress and fulfillment of this glorious covenant initiated with Abraham. As we observe the history of the covenant of grace, we will simultaneously see the development of the redemptive kingdom from its seed form in the days of Abraham until it comes to full expression in the first and second comings of Christ.

As I mentioned at the beginning of this section, Scripture portrays Abraham as living a two-kingdoms way of life. While Abraham's experience was certainly not identical to Christians' experience today, there is much that we must learn from it. As a descendant of Noah he lived under the parameters of the Noahic covenant and hence participated in the common kingdom, but as the recipient of God's special promises in the covenant of grace he also participated in the redemptive kingdom. The stories about Abraham's life in Genesis 12–25 show that he managed to live as a citizen of two kingdoms by remaining radically separate from the world in his religious faith and worship but simultaneously engaging in a range of cultural activities in common with his pagan neighbors. Just by

---

[3]For a good recent treatment of the covenant of grace and its progress through redemptive history, see e.g., Michael Horton, *God of Promise: Introducing Covenant Theology* (Grand Rapids: Baker, 2006).

glancing through these chapters a reader can see that Abraham lived in various places among the inhabitants of Palestine. Though God had promised that one day his descendants would possess the entire land, in the meantime Abraham and his household could not be identified with any particular geographical location, but lived as "sojourners" and "strangers" among pagans (Gen. 12:10; 15:13; 20:1; 21:34; 23:4; Heb. 11:13).

As he sojourned in the land, Abraham did not set up his own cultural ghetto but freely participated in his neighbors' cultural activities. Four particular activities illustrate this. First, Abraham participated in the military conflicts of the ancient Near East. In Genesis 14 a war breaks out among the local kings, and when his nephew Lot is captured by one group of kings, Abraham and the men of his household defeat them and rescue Lot. Second, Abraham participated in his pagan neighbors' commercial life. After Sarah's death, for example, Abraham approaches the Hittites who live nearby. He asks to buy a plot of land in order to bury Sarah and, after they negotiate a price, the Hittites deed the field to Abraham for his possession (Genesis 23).

Third, Abraham engaged in moral and judicial disputes with his pagan neighbors, and even came to mutually acceptable resolutions with them. An excellent example is the story of Abraham's encounter with Abimelech in Genesis 20. While living near Gerar, Abraham had told people that Sarah was his sister, and Abimelech the king of Gerar took her as his wife. Abimelech then confronts Abraham for his deception, which had created an adulterous situation and provoked God's displeasure. Abimelech the pagan rebukes Abraham the man of God, accusing him of doing things "that ought not to be done" (20:9; see vv. 9–10). Abraham counters with a partial defense. Interestingly, Abraham does not deny that he has wronged Abimelech, but he explains why he lapsed into such behavior: he thought that there was no "fear of God" in Gerar and that he would be killed by Sarah's suitors (20:11). As it turns out, Abraham was wrong—there was a certain fear of God among the pagans of Gerar. Abraham and

Abimelech thus have a conversation of moral substance,[4] and in the end they come to an agreement on restitution and future relations that seems acceptable to both parties (20:14–18). What we see, then, is that in the life of the common kingdom believers should not be too quick to claim the moral high ground against unbelievers, since they will not always come out looking better. We also see that it is possible for believers and unbelievers to have serious moral conversations with each other and to settle legal disputes in just and mutually beneficial ways.

Fourth, Abraham even entered into covenants with civil rulers of the lands in which he lived. The story narrated in Genesis 21:22–34 bears resemblance to the story of Abraham and Abimelech in Genesis 20. This time Abraham comes to Abimelech and complains to him about a property dispute, and again they exchange their views and come to an acceptable resolution (21:25–30). In this encounter, however, the two men, a believer and an unbeliever, swear oaths to one another and enter into a "covenant" (the same Hebrew word used for God's covenants with Noah and Abraham) (21:23–24, 32). In the affairs of the common kingdom, therefore, the believer enters into a close political alliance with a pagan prince, despite the radical spiritual antithesis that separates them.

In the generations that follow, Isaac, Jacob, and Jacob's children continue to live as sojourners in the land according to the general pattern established by Abraham. Things do not always go smoothly, of course, as the rape of Dinah (Genesis 34) and the enslavement of Joseph (Genesis 37) illustrate. But Joseph, evidently a godly man who retained his religious faith (see Gen. 39:11–12; 50:24–25), was even able to serve Pharaoh, king of Egypt, who claimed to be a god, and the descendants of Israel as a whole were able to prosper for many years living as sojourners in a new land, Egypt (Ex. 1:6–7).

Here, then, is a major clue as to what Christian life in the two kingdoms ought to look like today. Abraham and his descendants

---

[4]For discussion of this dialogue as a moral conversation, see David Novak, *Natural Law in Judaism* (Cambridge: Cambridge University Press, 1998), chap. 2; and David VanDrunen, *A Biblical Case for Natural Law* (Grand Rapids: Acton Institute, 2006), 42–49.

were "sojourners" and "strangers" (Gen. 12:10; 15:13; 20:1; 21:34; 23:4; Heb. 11:13), precisely what Christians today are called to be (1 Pet. 2:11). As participants in the Noahic covenant, they joined in cultural activities with their pagan neighbors in the common kingdom. As participants in the Abrahamic covenant, they were simultaneously citizens of the redemptive kingdom, remaining radically separate from their neighbors in their religious commitment as they trusted in the true God for justification (Gen. 15:6) and eternal life (Heb. 11:13–16).

The Two Kingdoms and the Mosaic Covenant

After the accounts of Abraham, Isaac, Jacob, and Joseph that extend through the end of Genesis, a new era in redemptive history opens with the book of Exodus. The people of Israel, now a great multitude but enslaved by the Egyptians, are delivered from their bondage and enter into a covenant with God on Mount Sinai, where they receive the law to regulate their new relationship with him. The rest of the Old Testament is about this covenant and how things transpire in the relationship between God and Israel through the following centuries. What does the Mosaic covenant teach us about the two kingdoms?

For one thing, Old Testament Israel under the Mosaic covenant teaches us much about the redemptive kingdom. As a "kingdom of priests and a holy nation" (Ex. 19:6; see vv. 5–6), Israel was the manifestation of the redemptive kingdom during the time between Moses and Christ. Many features of this kingdom were revealed in Israel that were not so clearly revealed during the days of Abraham. In Israel God raised up kings, foreshadowing Jesus, the true and everlasting king of the redemptive kingdom. In Israel God established a priesthood and a temple, again foreshadowing the ministry of Jesus, the Great High Priest, in his sacrificial death and heavenly intercession for his people. God also set apart a special land flowing with milk and honey for Israel, foreshadowing the eternal city of God. Old Testament Israel was not, to be sure, the final manifestation of the redemptive kingdom. God did not design the Mosaic law to

Jesus: Everlasting King, The great high Priest, Eternal city be permanent, but to serve as a "guardian," a teacher pointing the people to Christ (Gal. 3:19–24).[5]

For present purposes it is also crucial to note that Israel's experience under the law of Moses in the Promised Land of Canaan was *not* meant to exemplify life under the *two* kingdoms. The cultural commonality among believers and unbelievers ordained in the Noahic covenant was suspended for Israel within the borders of the Promised Land. A few aspects of the life that God ordained for Israel demonstrate this point and illustrate how different things were for Israel in the Promised Land in comparison to the experience of Abraham many years before.

First, unlike Abraham, the Israelites were not sojourners in the land. The land was theirs. As God said to Israel when they first left Mount Sinai, "See, I have set the land before you. Go in and take possession of the land that the LORD swore to your fathers, to Abraham, to Isaac, and to Jacob, to give to them and to their offspring after them" (Deut. 1:8). They no longer wandered but had arrived at home. Second, though Israel was to show kindness to foreigners residing temporarily in Canaan (Deut. 10:18–19; 26:12–13), it was not to maintain a common cultural life with pagans in the Promised Land. Abraham had entered into political covenants with unbelieving rulers during the days of his sojourning in Palestine (Gen. 21:32), but in the law of Moses God strictly commanded Israel never to do this: "you shall make no covenant with them and show no mercy to them" (Deut. 7:2). In fact, Israel was to destroy the pagan nations who had been living in Palestine. The first part of Deuteronomy 7:2 reads: "when the LORD your God gives them over to you, and you defeat them, then you must devote them to complete destruction. . . ." Unlike Abraham, therefore, who made covenants, traded, and waged war *alongside* his pagan neighbors, Israel was to wipe them off the

---

[5]Moses himself predicts that Israel will be unable to keep the terms of the Mosaic law and as a consequence will be scattered in exile, where a new initiative of God will be necessary to restore them; see Deuteronomy 30:1–10. Looking back at the Mosaic covenant after the coming of Christ, the author of Hebrews declares that covenant "obsolete and growing old" (Heb. 8:13)—it had served its purpose.

face of the earth.[6] Third, the Mosaic law directly regulated many areas of general cultural life, often in minute detail. In the Abrahamic covenant, God demanded that Abraham and his household acknowledge and trust in him as the one true God and perform the sacramental rite of circumcision. But God gave no specific rules for Abraham to follow in regard to his economic or political life. That radically changes with the covenant at Sinai. The Mosaic law regulated matters as diverse as kingship (e.g., Deut. 17:14–20), commercial trade (e.g., Lev. 25:23–34; Deut. 25:13–16), agriculture (e.g., Ex. 23:10–11), and public health (e.g., Leviticus 14). The Mosaic law required the enforcement of justice in civil relations (e.g., Exodus 21–22). The Mosaic covenant, and hence the redemptive kingdom during Israel's tenure in the land, encompassed their general cultural life as well as their distinctive acts of religious devotion.

It is clear, therefore, that human cultural activities were very different under Moses from what they were under Abraham. Under the Mosaic covenant God evidently suspended the provisions of the Noahic covenant that ordained that ordinary cultural activities should be a common enterprise among believers and unbelievers alike. But it is fascinating to note that God suspended these provisions of the Noahic covenant only inside the borders of the Promised Land. Outside the borders cultural activities went on as before according to the Noahic provisions. When Israelites stepped outside of their borders or dealt with nations who lived outside the land, furthermore, they could once again make alliances and trade in common with the world (without, of course, substituting political alliances for their trust in God). Outside the boundaries of the Promised Land they were again to conduct themselves as citizens of two kingdoms.

A good example of this principle is found in Deuteronomy 20, where the Mosaic law regulates warfare differently inside and

---

[6]God's commands to do this can of course be troubling and difficult to understand. It seems best to interpret them as a foretaste and picture of the day of judgment, when the Noahic covenant will come to an end, the world will be destroyed with fire, and unbelievers will be condemned. As the conquest of the Promised Land marked the end of Israel's days of sojourning in the wilderness and began their possession of a land that offered a foretaste of heaven, so the day of judgment will mark the end of Christians' sojourning in this world and begin their possession of heaven itself.

outside the land. First the law gives instruction for waging war against "all the cities that are very far from you, which are not cities of the nations here" (20:15). Israel must offer terms of peace to such cities and, if they accept, can only put them to forced labor. If they do not accept the terms and war ensues, Israel is to kill the males but take the women, children, livestock, and everything else as plunder (20:10–14). This, we might say, is warfare based on the reality of cultural commonality among all people under the Noahic covenant—it aims for peace if possible and limits the victor's harsh treatment of the vanquished. But Israel was to treat "the cities of these peoples that the LORD your God is giving you for an inheritance" in a very different way. Among these cities in Canaan "you shall save alive nothing that breathes, but you shall devote them to complete destruction . . ." (20:16–17). Another good example of the principle is the friendly relations that Solomon had with rulers of nations that lived outside Israel's borders. Solomon, at the height of his reign, dealt cordially with Hiram king of Tyre (1 Kings 5) and the queen of Sheba (1 Kings 10:1–13). Remarkably, Solomon acknowledged to Hiram that "there is no one among us who knows how to cut timber like the Sidonians" (5:6). Even in the heyday of the Old Testament theocracy Israel's pagan neighbors could still best them in this cultural activity. Solomon also carried on extensive commercial trade with various nations far away (1 Kings 10:22).

These examples, by their very contrast to what the Mosaic law generally says about how Israelites were to act toward non-Israelites, demonstrate how greatly different life under the Mosaic covenant was to be in the Promised Land, in comparison to Abraham's two-kingdoms way of life. In Israel's long history between the giving of the law to Moses and the coming of Christ, they nevertheless had one corporate experience which did exemplify the life of the two kingdoms: the Babylonian exile. Since the New Testament calls Christians "exiles" (1 Pet. 1:1, 17; 2:11) who are living in "Babylon" (Revelation 18), it is important that we examine Israel's experience in Babylon before concluding this chapter.

Exile in Babylon: The Two Kingdoms Once Again

In the previous section I noted that Israelites were to treat non-Israelites living outside the Promised Land differently from the way they were to treat those living inside the Promised Land. What would happen, then, if Israel *en masse* was to leave the Promised Land and live outside of it? This is precisely what occurred in the Babylonian exile. As we might expect, God instructed the exiles to live in Babylon as sojourners. They were to conduct themselves in ways similar to Abraham. The two kingdoms were again operative for God's covenant people.

A letter from Jeremiah contains the most explicit instructions that God gave to the exiles about how to conduct themselves in Babylon (Jeremiah 29). The beginning of this letter may sound rather mundane to us today, but it must have been shocking and almost appalling for godly Israelites. For the Israelites, we must remember, living in the Promised Land was not something they could take or leave. It was crucial to their life under the Mosaic covenant. To lose possession of the Promised Land was a curse of epic proportions (see Deut. 28:64–68). These exiles looked upon their Babylonian masters with fear and loathing (Psalm 137). What were they to do in the midst of this utter disaster and potential loss of their religious identity as the special people of God? False prophets were telling them that their exile would be short (Jer. 28:1–4), which may well have encouraged them to rebel and fight against the Babylonians. This background indicates why Jeremiah's letter must have been such a jolt to the exiles. Jeremiah instructs them to build houses, plant gardens, get married, and have children—"multiply there, and do not decrease" (29:6). In other words, they were to live peaceful lives and pursue ordinary cultural activities in this foreign land. If this was not a surprise enough, Jeremiah next writes: "seek the welfare of the city where I have sent you into exile, and pray to the LORD on its behalf, for in its welfare you will find your welfare" (29:7). What an amazing command for Israelites trained under the Mosaic law to hear! They were not simply to pursue ordinary cultural activities while they were in Babylon but were to *seek the welfare* of the pagan nation that ransacked the Holy Land and to *pray for it*. Their welfare was to be bound up with the welfare of their Babylonian hosts.

What was going on here? These instructions certainly could not be mistaken for a repetition of the Mosaic law. The Mosaic law used almost exactly the opposite language to teach Israel how to deal with foreigners in the Promised Land. For example, God had commanded with regard to Moabites and Ammonites: "You shall not seek their peace or their prosperity all your days forever" (Deut. 23:6). It was as if God purposely used language in Jeremiah 29 that would signal that things were going to be very different in exile. What the instructions in Jeremiah 29 sound like is what we would expect of people living under the Noahic covenant of Genesis 9, or of people looking back to Abraham's way of life as their model. They were not to pursue their cultural labors physically separated from or economically and politically distinguished from the cultural life of their pagan neighbors. Their cultural life would now be intertwined with that of unbelievers. They would inevitably prosper or suffer with the rising or sinking fortunes of the city in which they dwelled. They would live in a land without truly being able to claim it as their own. As Abraham sojourned among the Canaanites and Hittites as a fellow participant in the common kingdom, so the Israelite exiles were to sojourn among the Babylonians as fellow participants of the common kingdom.

Yet it is very important to note that the exile was truly a *two*-kingdoms experience for Israel. They participated in the common kingdom alongside Babylonians under the provisions of the Noahic covenant. But they were also radically separated from the Babylonians as the children of Abraham who still participated in the redemptive kingdom. Whatever cultural commonality they now shared with the Babylonians, they were also to maintain a radical spiritual antithesis. As with Abraham, cultural commonality was not meant to compromise their religious allegiance to the true God. Jeremiah goes on in his letter to prophesy a time when Israel would "call upon me and come and pray to me, and I will hear you. You will seek me and find me . . ." (29:12–13). God had continued to set apart Israel as a special people distinct from the other people of the world: "I know the plans I have for you, declares the LORD, plans for your welfare and not for evil, to give you a future and a hope" (29:11). Preachers today often take these familiar words out of context and apply them to Christians' ordinary cultural activities, as if God promises to prosper them in their work and finances. But the "hope" and "future" that God speaks of here is not in regard to their ordinary cultural activities in Babylon but *the end of their exile* and their *return to the Promised Land* after seventy years (29:10, 14; Deut. 30:1–3).

The basic picture becomes clear. For a period of seventy years the Israelites were to live in exile in Babylon, pursuing ordinary cultural activities and seeking the welfare of the very people who had destroyed the Promised Land. But they were to remain distinct from the Babylonians in their religious commitment to the true God and to maintain their hope of returning to Canaan. They were to build homes and plant gardens even though they could not keep these things. At the end of the seventy years, they would leave their homes and gardens behind and be restored to the Promised Land. Their time in Babylon was thus a time both of loving and serving their Babylonian hosts and of longing for the day of Babylon's destruction: they prayed for the peace and prosperity of Babylon while they simultaneously prayed: "O daughter of Babylon, doomed to be destroyed, blessed shall he be who repays you with what you have done to us! Blessed shall he be who takes your little ones and dashes them against the rock!" (Ps. 137:8–9).

The Old Testament not only records God's specific instructions to the exiles in Jeremiah 29 but also provides some concrete illustrations of how godly Israelite exiles actually lived, particularly in the book of Daniel. At the beginning of this book Daniel and his three friends—Shadrach, Meshach, and Abednego—come into the service of the Babylonian king Nebuchadnezzar. Nebuchadnezzar commanded that these men be educated in "the literature and language of the Chaldeans" (1:4), and they excelled in their studies (1:17). Upon completing their education they "stood before the king" (1:19) and became important officials in his kingdom. These remarkable events show that these men of God were taking Jeremiah's letter very seriously. Jeremiah commanded the exiles to carry out ordinary cultural activities in Babylon such as marrying, having children, building houses, and planting gardens, and Daniel and his friends even let themselves be educated in Babylonian schools and become Babylonian political officials (serving the king who destroyed Jerusalem). Jeremiah instructed them to "seek the welfare" of Babylon, and thus Daniel and his friends do not lead culturally isolated lives but participate in education and politics in common with the Babylonians. Babylon was part of the common kingdom established by God in the Noahic covenant, and thus believers in the true God could participate in its cultural life.

Two significant things stand out about the way in which Daniel and his friends conduct themselves as they participate so intimately in Babylonian public life. First, they never attempt to turn Babylon into something other than Babylon. They never try, for example, to turn Babylon into another Jerusalem or to impose the Mosaic law upon the Babylonian people. Babylon was part of the common kingdom, and they did not try to turn it into the redemptive kingdom founded upon the covenant with Abraham. It is interesting to note that when God judges kings Nebuchadnezzar and Belshazzar, he condemns them not for failing to keep the Mosaic law or for failing to believe in the saving promises given to Abraham. Instead, God condemns them for their *pride* (Dan. 4:30–32, 34–35; 5:20–23)— they lacked a sense of the "fear of God" exhibited by Abimelech, a pagan king with a refined sense of justice (see Gen. 20:11).[7] A city such as Babylon could not administer salvation, but by virtue of the Noahic covenant it was supposed to ensure some measure of justice

---

[7]The events described in Daniel 3:29; 4:37; and 6:26–27 raise interesting questions about Kings Nebuchadnezzar and Darius and their relationship to the true God and his worship. It is difficult to draw firm conclusions, since the biblical text does not clearly indicate whether these kings were genuinely converted or whether their actions should be models for civil rulers today. These kings did not, in any case, command anything distinctive to the redemptive kingdoms administered through the Abrahamic and Mosaic covenants, and thus did not impose *true* religious worship upon the pagan nations. In my judgment, their actions may be comparable to those of Abimelech in Genesis 20, who did not share in God's redemptive covenant through Abraham, yet was implicitly commended for governing in "the fear of God." Along similar lines are Daniel's words to Nebuchadnezzar in Daniel 4:27, where he exhorts the king to practice righteousness and show mercy to the oppressed, which are general duties of all civil rulers (see Rom. 13:3–4).

and civilization among its inhabitants. Daniel and his friends serve God, therefore, by *serving Babylon*, not by trying to transform it into a New Jerusalem.

Second, though Daniel and his friends were intimately involved in Babylonian public life, they would not compromise their higher allegiance to God or give up the hope that they possessed as citizens of the redemptive kingdom. The spiritual antithesis ran strong in their veins. On several occasions they refused to follow the instructions of the king when it meant defiling themselves with food forbidden by the Mosaic law, practicing idolatry, or praying to someone other than the one true God (see Dan. 1:8–16; 3:1–30; 6:1–28)—even at the risk of death in a fiery furnace or a lions' den. Studying in a Babylonian university and serving in the Babylonian royal court themselves were perfectly legitimate activities (as they implicitly fulfilled God's commands in Jer. 29:5–7), but if these activities demanded breaking commands of God, then Daniel and his friends would not compromise. In addition, Daniel never forgot where his true citizenship was. He not only followed Jeremiah's instructions about how to live in Babylon, but he also remembered Jeremiah's prophecy that after seventy years the Israelites would return to Jerusalem, and he earnestly begged God to keep his promise (Dan. 9:1–19). Sometimes it must have been tempting for Daniel, having attained a position of great power and influence in Babylon, to want to stay there. Yet he remained eager to give up everything he had attained in Babylon for the sake of returning to his true homeland.

The portrayal of life in exile in the book of Esther points in a similar direction as Daniel. When the Israelites' existence was threatened by Haman and King Ahasuerus, they responded not by rising up in holy war against the pagan enemy but by peaceful appeal to the king through Esther, and Esther herself does not ask for special treatment of the Jews based upon their unique covenant privileges. The Israelites end up killing many of their enemies, but they do so only upon orders from the pagan king and in self-defense (see Est. 8:9–14; 9:1–16). Scripture also says that the godly Israelite Nehemiah, while still in exile, served the Persian King as cupbearer (Neh. 1:11), an important position in the royal court.

Conclusion

This chapter has traced the emergence of the spiritual antithesis between believers and unbelievers and the origin of the two kingdoms in the Old Testament. God is the one King of both kingdoms, but he rules them in different ways. He rules the common kingdom through the Noahic covenant, maintaining order in the natural world and ordaining a social order that encompasses all people, whether believers or unbelievers. He rules the redemptive kingdom through the covenant of grace formalized with Abraham, bestowing salvation upon believers and setting them apart from the world in a holy community of faith and worship. The two kingdoms have distinct natures and serve distinct purposes in this world, but both of them operate under God's sovereign moral authority. Both kingdoms have been created by divine covenant, and God commissions believers to serve him in both.

At the end of this study of Old Testament teaching it may be helpful to recall which Old Testament imagery the New Testament uses to describe Christians' identity in the present world. The New Testament never identifies any place where Christians live as a promised land and never describes Christians as those who can claim any place as their possession. Heaven is the only Promised Land for Christians. The New Testament calls Christians "exiles" and "sojourners" living in the *diaspora*, that is, in "dispersion" (James 1:1; 1 Pet. 1:1, 17; 2:11). They are not like Israelites living in separation from the world in their own homeland but are like Abraham and like the Israelites in Babylon who lived in a land and participated in a culture to which they did not ultimately belong (Heb. 11:8–16; Revelation 18). As Abraham or Daniel could have said, "here we have no lasting city" (Heb. 13:14). It is now time to explore in detail how the two-kingdoms theme, so powerfully exemplified in Abraham and the Babylonian exiles, comes to expression in the New Testament, especially in light of the coming of Christ, the proclamation of the kingdom of heaven, and the establishment of the church.

New Testament Sojourners

ON THREE DIFFERENT OCCASIONS Peter refers to Christians as "exiles" and/or "sojourners" (1 Pet. 1:1, 17; 2:11). One of Peter's chief concerns is to instruct Christians about their place in the present world, and he indicates that New Testament believers will have an experience similar to that of Abraham and the Babylonian exiles. Unlike the Israelites in the Promised Land under the Mosaic covenant, Christians are not called to be separated from unbelievers in an earthly homeland, but to live in lands that are not their own, where they live adjacent to unbelievers and work alongside them. Like Abraham and the Babylonian exiles they have been radically distinguished from the world by their faith and worship of the one true God and by their hope of possessing a homeland. But in this world they intermingle with unbelievers, sharing many cultural activities in common with them even while striving not to share in their sins. Spiritual antithesis and cultural commonality are still the order of the day.

At the same time, the experience of New Testament believers is also very different from—and much better than—that of Abraham and the Babylonian exiles. Old Testament believers were indeed true saints who enjoyed the same salvation that Christians enjoy today. Abraham trusted God, was justified by faith, and put his hope not in an earthly Promised Land but in a heavenly and eternal Promised Land (Gen. 15:6; Romans 4; Heb. 11:8–19). The Old Testament believers, however, experienced these blessings only as they looked in anticipation to the coming of the Messiah, the last Adam. Abraham rejoiced to see the day of Christ, but he could only see it from a distance (John 8:56). The Israelites had priests, sacrifices, and a temple that were only shadows of the greater and perfect sacrifice of Jesus the Great High Priest (Hebrews 7–10). With the coming of Christ Christians now can see things so much more clearly. We look back upon the completed work of Christ the last Adam—his life, death, resurrection, and ascension. He has fulfilled the task of the first Adam and entered into Adam's original destiny, the world-to-come (Heb. 2:5–9). There he sits as our Great High Priest, who has offered a sufficient sacrifice for sin once and for all and lives forever to intercede for us (Heb. 7:25; 10:12). He has poured out his Holy Spirit upon us (Acts 2:33) and given us access to the heavenly sanctuary in the eternal temple (Heb. 4:16; 10:19–22). While the Old Testament saints saw the world-to-come from a very far distance, New Testament saints share in its life most intimately and stand on the very precipice of eternity (Phil. 3:19–20; Col. 3:1–4).

Part of the blessing of these last days is that believers are members of the New Testament church. The Old Testament worshiping communities were confined to one family (in the days of Abraham) or to one ethnic nation (under Moses and in the days of the Babylonian exile). They existed in only one geographical area and exercised no missionary task to speak of. After the coming of Christ the church is composed of people "from every tribe and language and people and nation" (Rev. 5:9) in which "there is not Greek and Jew, circumcised and uncircumcised, barbarian, Scythian, slave, free . . ." (Col. 3:11). They live spread over the world, even to "the end of the earth" (Acts 1:8), and the missionary task is central to her identity (Matt. 28:19–20). The church is the body of Christ (1 Cor. 12:27), the household of God (1 Tim. 3:15), the very gateway to the kingdom of heaven (Matt. 16:18–19). Though the church today is clothed in weakness and humility it is far more glorious than anything the Old Testament saints ever experienced.

Few things are more important for the two-kingdoms doctrine than a proper view of the kingdom of God that Jesus announced. In this chapter I will defend a crucial claim: the church is the *only* institution or community in the present world that can be identified with the kingdom proclaimed by Christ. In the work of Christ and the establishment of the church, God has brought the covenant with Abraham and the redemptive kingdom to penultimate fulfillment.[1]

Yet the church exists as a community of sojourners and exiles precisely because the common kingdom, founded in the Noahic covenant, continues to exist. God promised that the Noahic covenant would endure "while the earth remains" (Gen. 8:22), and he has kept his word. Work, family life, the pursuit of justice, and all sorts of other cultural activities continue to exist among all people, believers and unbelievers, and New Testament Christians are called to share much in common culturally with their non-Christian neighbors. Christians must strive for faithful obedience to God in both kingdoms. On the one hand, they must serve God in the worship, fellowship, and mission of the church as the redemptive kingdom now made manifest in this world. On the other hand, they must serve God and neighbor in the many cultural activities of the common kingdom. In both kingdoms they render loving obedience to the one true God, yet do so in different ways.

Exploring these themes is the purpose of this chapter. I begin by focusing on the redemptive kingdom and discussing how this kingdom and the covenant with Abraham have come to penultimate fulfillment in the work of Christ and the establishment of his church. Then I turn to the common kingdom and observe how the Noahic covenant continues to be operative in the present world and how Christians should participate in its activities and institutions. Toward the end of this chapter I reflect upon the attitude and perspective that Christians should cultivate as they seek both to

---

[1] I write "penultimate" fulfillment because, as mentioned again below, their "ultimate" fulfillment awaits the second coming of Christ and the revelation of the new heaven and new earth.

live in cultural commonality with the world and to maintain their spiritual antithesis with unbelievers and their great hope of life in the world-to-come.

The Redemptive Kingdom and the Church of Jesus Christ

In chapter 4 I introduced the *redemptive kingdom*. I argued that the redemptive kingdom originated in the covenant of grace that was formally established through the covenant promises made to Abraham in Genesis 15 and 17. The New Testament narrates how the covenant of grace and the redemptive kingdom find their ultimate fulfillment in the world-to-come. God will bring the covenant relationship to perfection, for he "will dwell with them, and they will be his people, and God himself will be with them as their God" (Rev. 21:3). In doing so, he will bring the kingdom to perfection, for the new heaven and new earth will be "the holy city, new Jerusalem," populated by the blessed saints who are "the kings of the earth" (Rev. 21:2, 24).

Until that day of ultimate fulfillment, the covenant of grace and the redemptive kingdom find their penultimate fulfillment in the church of the Lord Jesus Christ. When Christ came, he did not establish the state, or the family, or a school, or a business venture. These things already existed and were governed and preserved under the covenant with Noah. The Lord Jesus Christ established one thing: his church.[2] According to the New Testament, the redemptive kingdom and the covenant of grace come to their fullest earthly expression in the church, and in the church alone. It is true, of course, that Christians are citizens of this kingdom and members of this covenant at all times. They should live obedient lives to Christ in every aspect of life and should manifest the power of Christ's kingdom and covenant in all they do. But the church is the *only* institution and community in this world that can be identified with the redemptive kingdom and the covenant of grace.

---

[2]When I refer to the "church" in this and the following chapters, I am generally referring to the *New Testament* church. There is a certain sense in which "the church" existed even during the Old Testament, since God has always gathered and governed his people and since there is an organic continuity among God's people through all the ages, as the following pages explore.

This high view of the church sets the two-kingdoms vision of this book apart from many redemptive transformationist models dominant in contemporary conversations about Christianity and culture. In the next sections we will first consider the relationship of the church to the covenant of grace and then we will consider the relationship of the church to the kingdom of heaven that Jesus proclaimed.

The Fulfillment of the Abrahamic Covenant in the Church

God established his covenant of grace with Abraham in Genesis 15 and 17. While the covenant with Noah in Genesis 9 promised to preserve life in this world for all people and all creatures, the Abrahamic covenant embraced a particular people set apart from the world and promised them salvation and life in the world-to-come. The rest of the Old Testament looks back to the Abrahamic covenant as the foundation that underlies God's relationship with Israel. Despite Israel's great sin, God continued to remember his covenant with Abraham. This was Israel's chief source of assurance that God would not totally reject them (e.g., Ex. 32:11–14). The New Testament announces that until this covenant of grace comes to ultimate fulfillment in the new heaven and new earth, it finds penultimate fulfillment in the work of Christ and his church. The church, united to Christ its Savior, is the covenant community that reaps the benefits of Christ's work in fulfilling the promises made to Abraham. In the present day the church, and no other institution, can claim this privilege. The church is the community where salvation and eternal life are bestowed. Galatians 3 and Ephesians 2–3 provide a bird's-eye view of this truth.

Before Paul arrives at his discussion of the Abrahamic covenant in Galatians 3, he begins his epistle with two important statements. First, he greets his audience as "the *churches* of Galatia" (1:2). Paul's letter does not address other institutions of society, but addresses churches (and individual Christians insofar as they are members of these churches). Second, Paul proceeds to give a blessing to the churches, and he mentions two acts of Christ in particular. Christ "gave himself for our sins" in order to "deliver us from the present evil age . . ." (1:4). These are precisely the blessings of the Abrahamic covenant identified above: forgiveness of sins through justification and deliverance from this present evil age through citizenship in the world-to come. Thus Paul, in these opening verses of Galatians, gives an initial hint that the promises of the Abrahamic covenant are being fulfilled in the church through the work of Christ.

Galatians 3 explicitly develops this theme. Paul not only explains why the New Testament church is no longer under the covenant with Moses but also affirms that Christians in the church are participants in the earlier covenant with Abraham. The "sons of Abraham" who receive "the blessing of Abraham" are those who have faith in Christ (3:7, 14; see v. 9). This is because God's promises "to Abraham and to his offspring" were ultimately to Abraham and *Christ* (3:16). The fulfillment of the Abrahamic covenant is found in the Lord Jesus. People with a faith like Abraham's belong to Christ and thus have a share in the Abrahamic covenant (3:6–9, 14, 22). "In Christ Jesus you are all sons of God, through faith. For as many of you as were baptized into Christ have put on Christ. . . . And if you are Christ's, then you are Abraham's offspring, heirs according to promise" (3:26–27, 29). Of course not every baptized person has true faith in Christ, but for Paul, as a general matter, the people of faith are those who have been set apart by baptism, and the community of the baptized is *the church*. Paul keeps speaking of "you" and "we" as the heirs of Abraham in Galatians 3 because he is addressing "the churches of Galatia" (1:2). The church, as the community of the baptized, claims the promises of the Abrahamic covenant. No other earthly institution or organization is identified by the mark of baptism, and thus none of them can claim these promises.

Paul also explains this connection between the Old Testament covenant promises and the New Testament church in Ephesians 2:11–3:13. At one time Gentiles were "separated from Christ, alienated from the commonwealth of Israel and strangers to the covenants of promise, having no hope and without God in the world" (2:12). Paul does not mention Abraham by name, but Galatians 3 makes clear that the covenant with Abraham was *the* "covenant of promise" in the Old Testament. Thus, Ephesians 2 means that Gentiles formerly did not participate in the Abrahamic covenant and its promises (and hence did not belong to Christ or to the commonwealth of Israel). But the work of Christ has radically changed this state of affairs (2:13–18). Christ has removed "the law of commandments and ordinances" and has made "us both [Jew and Gentile] one." Gentiles and Jews alike are now participants in the Old Testament covenants of promise.

They participate in these promises because they are "fellow citizens with the saints and members of the household of God, built on the foundation of the apostles and prophets, Christ Jesus himself being the cornerstone, in whom the whole structure, being joined together, grows into a holy temple in the Lord" (Eph. 2:19–21). For Paul, these are simply various ways of talking about the *church*: the church is the household of God (1 Tim. 3:15), the building founded upon Christ and the apostles (1 Cor. 1:2; 3:5–15), the holy temple of the New Testament (1 Cor. 3:16–17; 2 Cor. 1:1; 6:16). In case there is any doubt, Paul says it explicitly in Ephesians 3. The "mystery of Christ" is "that the Gentiles are fellow heirs, members of the *same body*, and *partakers of the promise in Christ Jesus* through the gospel" (Eph. 3:4–6), and this "mystery" has been brought to light "so that through *the church* the manifold wisdom of God might now be made known . . ." (Eph. 3:10; see vv. 9–10).

The blessings of the Old Testament covenant promises, first delivered to Abraham, are now enjoyed in the church. No other earthly institution can claim to be the household of God, a holy temple, or the body of Christ. Christ died for *the church*: "Christ loved the church and gave himself up for her, that he might sanctify her, having cleansed her by the washing of water with the word, so that he might present the church to himself in splendor, without spot or wrinkle or any such thing, that she might be holy and without blemish" (Eph. 5:25–27). Such love is the model for a husband's love for his wife (5:25–33)—it is intimate, special, and reserved for her alone. What great and unique privileges the church enjoys!

According to Paul, therefore, the church is the only contemporary institution or community that can lay claim to the promises of the

Abrahamic covenant.[3] The church is where the blessings of salvation are bestowed, where there is "neither Jew nor Greek, there is neither slave nor free, there is no male and female, for you are all one in Christ Jesus" (Gal. 3:28). It is where the Abrahamic covenant continues in a much grander way, for here is made known "the mystery of Christ, which was not made known to the sons of men in other generations as it has now been revealed . . ." (Eph. 3:4–5). In the church we know and experience so many things to which Abraham could only look forward.

The Coming of the Kingdom of Heaven
In chapter 4 I claimed that the redemptive kingdom was formally established in the Abrahamic covenant. Therefore, if the Abrahamic covenant finds its present expression and fulfillment in the church, so must the redemptive kingdom. In the next two sections we will explore how the New Testament teaches that the redemptive kingdom finds its present manifestation and penultimate fulfillment in the church, and the church alone.

The redemptive "kingdom" was initially tiny, just a single household. Yet God promised Abraham: "I will make you into nations, and kings shall come from you" (Gen.17:6). After turning Abraham's descendants into a numerous people, God entered into another covenant with them at Sinai and proclaimed them "a kingdom of priests and a holy nation . . ." (Ex. 19:6). In the covenant with David God promised that he would "establish the throne of his kingdom forever" (2 Sam. 7:13). What has become of this redemptive kingdom now that Christ has come and the promises to Abraham are being fulfilled? Jesus, the "son of David" (Matt. 1:1), announced the coming of the kingdom of God and pointed to the church as the community where the power of the kingdom resides (Matt. 16:18–19). Thus today it is *Christians*, the New Testament "exiles and sojourners," who are "a chosen race, a royal priesthood, a holy nation, a people for his own

---

[3]It is important to remember that though the family is an institution of the common kingdom—founded at creation (Gen. 2:18–25) and maintained in the Noahic covenant (Gen. 9:1, 7), enjoyed by believer and unbeliever alike—the redemptive kingdom makes special use of the family in bestowing saving blessings upon God's people (e.g., Gen. 17:7; Acts 2:39; Eph. 6:4). See further discussion about the New Testament's teaching on the family later in this chapter.

possession . . ." (1 Pet. 2:9–11). Perhaps no New Testament book makes these points as clear as the Gospel of Matthew.

The kingdom makes a spectacular first impression in Matthew. The very terminology is impressive—it is the kingdom of *heaven*. The other three Gospels typically use the term "kingdom of God" to describe the same kingdom, but Matthew's terminology signals that this kingdom has broken into this world from the world-to-come.[4] As Jesus states elsewhere, "my kingdom is not of this world . . ." (John 18:36). In proclaiming a kingdom not of this world Jesus does things that are, we might say, out of this world. He performs miraculous healings, his fame spreads everywhere, and huge crowds come out to follow him (Matt. 4:23–25).

Another striking thing about this kingdom early in Matthew is that it is something *new*. The kingdom that Jesus proclaims was prophesied and anticipated in the Old Testament, but something intrudes into this world such as the world has never seen before. It is significant that Jesus does not begin preaching about the kingdom of heaven until John the Baptist is arrested (4:12–17). John the Baptist was the last of the Old Testament prophets, the "Elijah who is to come" (11:14), as prophesied by Malachi (Mal. 4:5). "All the Prophets and the Law prophesied until John" (Matt. 11:13). When John was arrested, the era of the Old Testament prophets ended. John himself had prophesied that one greater than he was about to come (3:11–12), pointing to Jesus (3:13–17). Now that John has finished his ministry, the old is over and the new has come. To highlight the newness of his kingdom, Jesus begins teaching and healing in "Galilee *of the Gentiles*" (4:15). The kingdom of heaven belongs to Gentiles as well as to Jews. The Old Testament, the era of Moses, is coming to an end.

The Sermon on the Mount (Matthew 5–7) wonderfully illustrates how this new kingdom of heaven has surpassed the redemptive kingdom under the Old Testament and brought it to fulfillment.[5] Jesus is

---

[4]For an extensive recent argument that Matthew did not employ the term "kingdom of heaven" in order to avoid using the divine name so as not to offend his Jewish readers, see Jonathan T. Pennington, *Heaven and Earth in the Gospel of Matthew* (Leiden: Brill, 2007).

[5]For a more detailed argument for many claims made in this section, see David VanDrunen, "Bearing Sword in the State, Turning Cheek in the Church: A Reformed Two Kingdoms Interpretation of Matthew 5:38–42," *Themelios* 34 (November 2009): 322–34.

not just another religious teacher but one with profound authority. Before teaching, he "went up on the mountain" like Moses and "sat down" (5:1). By the time he finishes, "the crowds were astonished at his teaching, for he was teaching them as one who had authority, and not as their scribes" (7:28–29).

Being like Moses would be impressive enough, but the Sermon on the Mount reveals that Jesus is even *greater* than Moses. Jesus implicitly claims this about himself: "Do not think that I have come to abolish the Law or the Prophets; I have not come to abolish them but to fulfill them. For truly, I say to you, until heaven and earth pass away, not an iota, not a dot, will pass from the Law until all is accomplished" (5:17–18). It is interesting that Jesus would warn them in this way. Apparently some people saw Jesus' actions and heard his words and thought that he *was* abolishing Moses and the Old Testament—and this is very understandable given the power and the newness of his kingdom. Jesus is not abolishing Moses, however, and neither is he simply giving Moses a rubber stamp (as an initial reading of 5:19 might suggest). *Christ and his kingdom bring the Old Testament redemptive kingdom and its law to fulfillment.* Because the kingdom of heaven has arrived, God's people will no longer be under the redemptive kingdom of old. Yet the kingdom of old passes from the scene not as a despised relic of the past, but as an honored part of God's plan for history whose purposes have been accomplished now that Christ has come. God put the Mosaic law into effect temporarily as a guardian until the coming of Christ. When Christ comes, God's people can no longer be under the law (Gal. 3:24–25).

The rest of Matthew 5 illustrates that Jesus is neither reiterating nor abolishing the Mosaic law. Jesus gives a series of sayings, each of which begins with: "You have heard that it was said . . . but I say to you." The first few sayings make clear that he is not abolishing the law. The kingdom of heaven demands the same basic moral purity as the Mosaic law, and Jesus emphasizes just how profound this purity should be: the prohibitions of murder and adultery extend even to anger and lust (5:21–30). The final four sayings of Matthew 5, however, demonstrate that Jesus is not simply reiterating the

Old Testament law, but saying something different.[6] In contrast to Moses' rule, "whoever divorces his wife, let him give her a certificate of divorce," Jesus asserts: "everyone who divorces his wife, except on the ground of sexual immorality, makes her commit adultery . . ." (5:32). In contrast to Moses' command, "you shall not swear falsely, but shall perform to the Lord what you have sworn," Jesus commands: "do not take an oath at all . . ." (5:33–34). Over against Moses' principle, "an eye for an eye and a tooth for a tooth," Jesus teaches: "do not resist the one who is evil . . ." (5:38–39). While Moses said, "you shall love your neighbor and hate your enemy,"[7] Jesus says: "love your enemies . . ." (5:43–44).

Jesus is not simply repeating the Old Testament law. The life of his kingdom is new and, in certain respects, different from the life of the redemptive kingdom under Moses. This is especially clear with regard to questions of conflict and justice. As observed in chapter 4, the Mosaic covenant (in distinction from the Abrahamic covenant) gave detailed requirements about the legal and political life of God's people, and it prescribed a very strict form of justice: eye for an eye, tooth for a tooth.[8] When there was serious marital conflict, it provided a way for orderly divorce. When there was a judicial case, it required oaths to ensure that witnesses would tell the truth. When someone was convicted of a tort, it ordered a strict and proportionate penalty. When enemies of God and his people encroached upon the Promised Land, it commanded their destruc-

---

[6]Here I must differ with eminent biblical exegetes in my own Reformed tradition such as John Calvin and Herman Ridderbos, who see Jesus as primarily clarifying the demands of the Mosaic law, over against the twisting of the law by the Jewish authorities of his day. See John Calvin, *Commentary on a Harmony of the Evangelists, Matthew, Mark, and Luke*, vol. 1, trans. William Pringle (Grand Rapids: Baker, 2003), 281–83; and Herman Ridderbos, *The Coming of the Kingdom*, trans. H. de Jongste, ed. Raymond O. Zorn (Phillipsburg, NJ: P&R, 1962), chap. 7.

[7]I understand "hate your enemy" as a paraphrase of the Old Testament commands given to Israel through Joshua to exterminate the pagan nations living in Canaan.

[8]See Exodus 21:22–25; Leviticus 24:18–21; and Deuteronomy 19:21. This *lex talionis* was not necessarily meant to be implemented literally, though it did impose the important legal standard of proportionate justice. This legal standard has also been expressed in many other legal systems through history. On the *lex talionis* generally, see William Ian Miller, *Eye for an Eye* (Cambridge: Cambridge University Press, 2006). For a theological exploration of the idea, see David VanDrunen, "Natural Law, the *Lex Talionis*, and the Power of the Sword," *Liberty University Law Review* 2 (Spring 2008): 945–67.

tion. The Mosaic law exhorted Israel to love God and neighbor (Lev. 19:18; Deut. 6:5), but only in a way compatible with executing justice against the wrongdoer.

Things are very different in the kingdom of heaven. In this kingdom marital tension should not lead to divorce, lawsuits with oath-taking witnesses should not be necessary, slaps on the cheek should not provoke a proportionate retaliation, and the presence of an enemy should not enflame hatred. Instead, Jesus explains that his kingdom is about forgiveness, reconciliation, and restoration. What if someone "has something against you," "slaps you on the right cheek," or "persecutes you"? The response is not seeking justice but being "reconciled to your brother," not resisting the wrongdoer but turning the other cheek, and not hating your enemies but "loving your enemies" (Matt. 5:23, 39, 44). The kingdom of heaven is a realm where the demands of justice seem strangely transcended.

How does this *fulfill* the Law and the Prophets and not in fact *abolish* them? To answer this question we should remember that the Sermon on the Mount is not first and foremost about ethics, but about *Jesus himself*. He went up on the mountain to claim authority, and his authority was recognized by the people (5:1; 7:28–29). Jesus is the son of David, the true king of Israel (1:1). He "will save his people from their sins" (1:21) and "give his life as a ransom for many" (20:28). He resisted the temptations of Satan (4:1–11), rose up from the dead (28:5–6), and now claims "all authority in heaven and on earth" (28:18). In other words, he is the *last Adam*. He was faithful through temptation and now claims the rightful rule that the first Adam should have gained. The kingdom of heaven is therefore the kingdom of the world-to-come, which the first Adam would have attained if he had been obedient. It is the redemptive kingdom come to fulfillment.

These considerations should put the Sermon on the Mount in better perspective. The commands of the Sermon are not a universal human ethic meant for all people, but they are given only to those *who are already citizens* of the kingdom of heaven. Jesus actually teaches only his disciples (Matt. 5:1–2), and before giving them a single command he declares that they are "blessed," the "salt of the earth," and the "light of the world" (5:11, 13–14). He has won the kingdom for them once and for all. He satisfied the claims of justice, and thus he attained the first Adam's reward. Jesus' disciples, therefore, have entered a kingdom that does not seek justice but basks in the reality of justice satisfied. If they are citizens of the kingdom of heaven and thus lay claim to the kingdom originally intended for the first Adam, then justice has no more claims against them.[9] When someone wrongs them, they have the privilege not of seeking strict justice (returning a slap with a slap) but of showing forth the gospel. How interesting that Jesus tells them not to walk away when someone slaps them, but to turn the other cheek for a second slap. This is precisely what God in Christ has done for us who are citizens of his kingdom! Instead of returning the evil we did to him with a proportionate retaliation or simply walking away and ignoring us, God turned his other cheek, as it were, and endured a second evil from us by letting us crucify his Son. When the citizens of heaven refuse to retaliate against an evildoer, but instead endure the second evil themselves, they are a living exhibit of the gospel. This is not the *abolition* of the law and the claims of justice, but reflects their *fulfillment* in the work of Christ, just as Jesus said (5:17).

The kingdom of heaven, as the full flowering of the redemptive kingdom, is an amazing reality. It was the original goal of the first Adam, but now Christ the last Adam has become its king and made his people its citizens. In this kingdom Christians have nothing left to prove, no justice yet to achieve. Thus they pursue an ethic that exhibits the reconciliation and forgiveness that come in the gospel and forsake the claims of justice against those who wrong them.[10] No wonder that the New Testament calls them exiles and sojourners in this world and

---

[9] The Mosaic law reminded the Israelites of Adam's original requirements and pointed them ahead to the last Adam who had not yet come. The Mosaic law was in part a reminder that the claims of justice still had not been satisfied. The Israelites thus had to swear oaths and go to court, they had to repay eye for eye and tooth for tooth, and they had to strike down their enemies within the Promised Land. See David VanDrunen, "The Two Kingdoms and the *Ordo Salutis*: Life beyond Judgment and the Question of a Dual Ethic," *Westminster Theological Journal* 70 (Fall 2008): 207–24.

[10] See footnote 16 below for a brief discussion of whether self-defense or seeking retributive justice is ever permissible for Christians.

citizens of heaven. Living by the Sermon on the Mount means that they will certainly not feel at home in the present world.

The Church and the Kingdom of Heaven

Given these observations about the Sermon on the Mount and the kingdom of heaven, how exactly are Christians to put this new way of life into practice? Some theologians have suggested that Jesus was presenting an impossible ideal that really cannot be put into practice in the present world.[11] Others suggest that Jesus was speaking hyperbolically and thus not really prohibiting the quest for justice in all circumstances.[12] Still others press the literal force of Jesus' words and claim that Christians should embrace nonviolence and perhaps full-fledged pacifism.[13] This is a difficult issue, but I suggest two basic ideas as a guide for applying the various pieces of biblical evidence. First, Jesus intended his words to be put into practice in this world and, second, he intended his words not primarily as an individual ethic but as the ethic of a community—and *the church* was the community he had in mind.

To defend the claim that Jesus intended his words to be put into practice (and not merely admired as an unattainable ideal), I merely point out a few verses within the Sermon. Jesus emphasizes that his disciples are to *do* and *teach* his commandments (Matt. 5:19). He warns that only those who have *done* "the will of my Father" "will enter the kingdom of heaven" (7:21). And Jesus says that the wise man is the one "who hears these words of mine and does them . . ." (7:24). The precise application of his words may not always be easy to determine, but Christians must strive to obey them. This is a

---

[11]E.g., see Reinhold Niebuhr, *An Interpretation of Christian Ethics* (New York: Harper & Brothers, 1935), chap. 2.

[12]E.g., see Jan Lambrecht, S. J., "The Sayings of Jesus on Nonviolence," *Louvain Studies* 12, no. 4 (1987): 297–300.

[13]Many proponents of this, however, see their nonviolence not as a way to withdraw from broader society but as a way to transform it. E.g., see John Howard Yoder, *The Politics of Jesus: Vicit Agnus Noster* (Grand Rapids: Eerdmans, 1972); Richard B. Hays, *The Moral Vision of the New Testament: Community, Cross, New Creation; A Contemporary Introduction to New Testament Ethics* (New York: HarperSanFrancisco, 1996), 317–46; and Glen H. Stassen and David P. Gushee, *Kingdom Ethics: Following Jesus in Contemporary Context* (Downers Grove: InterVarsity, 2003), 132–40.

heavenly ethic meant to be put into practice in the midst of a world filled with sin and conflict.

But how and where? We must remember what the Sermon on the Mount is. Jesus is not a wise man passing along tips for better living to individuals who might be interested. He is describing the ethic of a *kingdom*. It is a *community's* way of life. The primary question to answer then is not *how am I* to put the Sermon into practice but *how are we* to put it into practice. (Secondarily, of course, the Sermon has implications for Christians individually.) We have not yet entered the New Jerusalem, so is there a community that exists here on earth in which we can experience and participate in the heavenly city ahead of time? Is there an earthly community in which the heavenly ethic of the Sermon is to be exemplified?

The Gospel of Matthew points to *the church*. After Peter confesses that Jesus is the Christ, the Son of the living God, Jesus blesses him and says: "And I tell you, you are Peter, and on this rock I will build my church, and the gates of hell shall not prevail against it. I will give you the keys of the kingdom of heaven, and whatever you bind on earth shall be bound in heaven, and whatever you loose on earth shall be loosed in heaven" (16:18–19). Jesus entrusts the keys of his kingdom to the church.[14] The church is the earthly entrance into the kingdom of heaven. If we have been reading Matthew carefully up to this point in his Gospel, we must be asking: where is the kingdom of heaven to be found? Jesus here points us to an earthly community that is the gateway to the kingdom.

Jesus makes this even more clear in Matthew 18, where he indicates that the ethic of the church is precisely the ethic of the kingdom of heaven described in the Sermon on the Mount. Jesus says: "If your brother sins against you, go and tell him his fault, between you and him alone. If he listens to you, you have gained your brother. But if he does not listen, take one or two others along with you, that every

---

[14]Two things may be helpful to note over against traditional Roman Catholic use of this text in support of the primacy of Peter and the office of the papacy. First, in Matthew 16:13–15 Jesus addresses the disciples collectively (in the plural), and thus Peter responds on behalf of them all. Second, the New Testament subsequently teaches that the apostles collectively (not Peter individually) are the foundation of the church, as they exercise their ministry on behalf of God's people (Eph. 2:19–22; 4:11–12).

charge may be established by the evidence of two or three witnesses. If he refuses to listen to them, tell it to the church. And if he refuses to listen even to the church, let him be to you as a Gentile and a tax collector. Truly, I say to you, whatever you bind on earth shall be bound in heaven, and whatever you loose on earth shall be loosed in heaven" (18:15–18). These last words, the same as those in Matthew 16, show that Jesus is again talking about the relationship of the kingdom and the church. The church is the community of the citizens of the kingdom, and when one "brother" sins against another, it is to follow the Sermon on the Mount. Instead of seeking strict justice against the sinner—eye for an eye and tooth for a tooth— Christians should make every possible effort to be reconciled with him and to restore him into the church's fellowship. If at any step along the way the sinner repents, that puts an end to the matter.[15] Gaining a just verdict against the sinner never enters the picture. Even if the sinner refuses to repent, the church does not take up the sword in vengeance but peacefully treats him as no longer one of its members. Matthew, in fact, emphasizes that when the church conducts itself in this way, it acts like its Lord. Immediately before this passage Matthew records the parable of the lost sheep (18:10–14) and immediately after this passage he records the parable of the unforgiving servant (18:21–35). The church, as the kingdom of heaven on earth, must imitate the Lord Jesus in seeking wandering sheep and forgiving them lavishly. Paul gives similar instructions about church discipline (1 Cor. 5:1–13; 2 Cor. 2:5–11).

In teaching these things about the church, Matthew also indicates that the kingdom of heaven is *not* to be found in the social-political communities of the broader world. Jesus praises the faith of a centurion (8:10), but seems to have no problem with the fact that he is a professional soldier, an inherently violent occupation. Christians may serve as soldiers on behalf of the *state* (see also Acts

---

[15]In saying that evidence of genuine repentance should bring an ecclesiastical disciplinary case to an end, I do not mean to say that the church should fail to exercise pastoral wisdom in reincorporating people into the life of the church and seeking to heal lingering wounds. Simply because a disciplinary procedure ends and forgiveness is granted does not mean that things are immediately back to normal, without the need for ongoing efforts to restore relationships and to guide the wayward in godly paths. See chapter 6 for further discussion.

10:1–11:18). Later the Pharisees ask about paying taxes to Caesar and give Jesus the perfect opportunity to abolish the state or at least to say that the state has to play by the rules of the kingdom of heaven. But instead Jesus acknowledges that the state—in this case, the Roman Empire—has legitimate authority to levy taxes (and thus to collect them by force) (Matt. 22:15–22). Paul says the same thing about taxes (Rom. 13:6–7) and also says that the state rightly bears "the sword" (Rom. 13:4). I will say more about the state and other social institutions a little later, but for now I simply note that Jesus commands only the church, never the state, to practice the ethic of the kingdom of heaven.[16]

The many other statements that the Gospels make about the kingdom of heaven always tell us something about the church. The kingdom of heaven is like a sower sowing seed (Matt. 13:1–23)—and thus the church preaches the gospel through its ministers (1 Tim. 3:1–7, 14–15). The kingdom of heaven is like a net cast into the sea to catch fish of every kind (Matt. 13:47–50)— and thus the church gathers in the lost "from every tribe and language and people and nation" (Rev. 5:9) into a community where it no longer matters whether one is a Jew, Greek, barbarian, or Scythian (Col. 3:11). The kingdom of heaven is like a mustard seed and leaven, which have small beginnings but enjoy exponential growth (Matt. 13:31–33)[17]—and thus the church has spread from Jerusalem to Judea to Samaria to the ends of the earth (Acts 1:8). The kingdom

---

[16]One question that arises is whether Christians, in their private lives, should refuse to pursue retributive justice against those who wrong them. Though I do not have space to argue this thoroughly here, it seems to me that Christians generally should not seek retribution when they are persecuted *as Christians*, for the sake of Christ and his church (though, following the example of Paul in Acts 22:25–29, they may appeal to civil magistrates for *relief* from their persecutors, which is not the same as seeking retribution against them). The wrongs described in Matthew 5:39–42, after all, are most likely persecutions against people because they are identified with Christ (5:11–12). When people wrong them not because of their faith but simply out of a general criminal motive, however, it seems to me that this is a civil dispute and thus that Christians may defend themselves and seek redress through the justice system that God himself has ordained. In other words, the first is a matter of identity in the redemptive kingdom and the latter concerns identity in the common kingdom.

[17]Some people point to these parables as proof that the kingdom extends to all cultural institutions and not simply the church. The text of Matthew, however, never asserts this. Such a view depends upon a preconceived view of what the kingdom is and is not derived from the text itself.

of God is like the prodigal son being welcomed back to his father's bosom after living in debauchery (Luke 15:11–32)—and the church is composed of those who used to be "sexually immoral, . . . idolaters, . . . adulterers, . . . men who practice homosexuality, . . . thieves, . . . the greedy, . . . drunkards, . . . revilers, . . . swindlers . . ." (1 Cor. 6:9–11). In this last passage Paul, sounding just like the Lord Jesus, explains how things ought to be in the "church" based upon the reality of the "kingdom of God" (1 Cor. 6:4, 9). He never says this about any other earthly community. Want to see the kingdom of heaven here and now? Look at a faithful church of the Lord Jesus Christ.

We saw earlier that the covenant with Abraham finds its ultimate fulfillment in the new heaven and new earth and its penultimate fulfillment in the church. We have now seen that the redemptive kingdom, which emerged from the Abrahamic covenant, also finds its ultimate fulfillment in the new heaven and new earth and its penultimate fulfillment in the church. The church is the kingdom of heaven here on earth. Though the church is not *identical* to the covenant of grace or the kingdom of heaven, it is precisely in the church that the covenant and kingdom are experienced until Christ returns.

What Is This Church?

I have been making some stupendous claims about the church. What do I mean by "the church"? In our colloquial speech we often use the term "church" in different ways—to refer to a building, or to a worshiping community, or to the aggregate of believing individuals known only to God. There is nothing necessarily wrong with using the term "church" to refer to different things, and there is some variation in how the New Testament uses the term. But for the most part the New Testament, and certainly the texts considered above, use "church" to refer to the visible community of believers and their children. This community is united particularly in worship and is instructed, governed, and served by ministers, elders, and deacons appointed for those tasks. To use a common theological phrase, the church in the New Testament is primarily "visible."

116

For example, when Paul speaks of the covenant of Abraham finding fulfillment in the churches of Galatia, these communities are marked out by *baptism,* a visible sacramental sign (Gal. 3:27). In Ephesians 2–3, where Paul writes about the Old Testament covenants of promise coming to fulfillment in the church, he refers to the church as a community where he and his fellow apostles and prophets have ministered (2:20; see also 1 Cor. 3:5–9) and which has experienced concrete reconciliation among Jew and Gentile (2:13–19; 3:6). As the "body of Christ" the church exists in the intimate fellowship and mutual service of its members (1 Corinthians 12), as the "household of God" it has overseers and deacons (1 Timothy 3), and as the "kingdom of heaven" it exercises the keys of the kingdom and disciplinary procedures (Matt. 16:18–19; 18:15–20). The earthly communities that can claim the promises of the covenant and the blessings of the kingdom are visible, faithful churches of Christ spread over this world.

Consequently, in the rest of this book I refer to the church as a community or institution. It will be important to keep in mind that, seeking to follow Scripture, I distinguish between the work and life of *the church* and the work and life of *individual believers* (or groups of believers) as they make their way in this world.[18] Believers and groups of believers do not constitute "the church" in everything they do.

The Common Kingdom after the Coming of Christ

We have now seen that the Abrahamic covenant of grace and the redemptive kingdom have come to a glorious state of fulfillment

---

[18]It seems to me that this distinction is not always made clear in books advocating a redemptive transformationist view of Christian cultural engagement; e.g., see Michael W. Goheen and Craig G. Bartholomew, *Living at the Crossroads: An Introduction to Christian Worldview* (Grand Rapids: Baker Academic, 2008), 129, 160. Some readers may be familiar with the distinction between the church as "institution" and the church as "organism" commonly associated with Abraham Kuyper's ecclesiology. For a brief description of Kuyper's distinction, see Peter S. Heslam, *Creating a Christian Worldview: Abraham Kuyper on Calvinism* (Grand Rapids: Eerdmans, 1998), 134–35. I do not find biblical evidence that "the church" announced and founded by Christ in Matthew 16 had to do with the organic church as that term is used in Kuyper's ecclesiology. Herman Bavinck also uses the institution-organism distinction, though in a more modest and biblical way than Kuyper, in *Reformed Dogmatics,* vol. 4, *Holy Spirit, Church, and New Creation,* ed. John Bolt, trans. John Vriend (Grand Rapids: Baker, 2008), 329–32.

with the coming of Christ, and we have seen that Christ established his church as the community where believers find the life and fellowship of that covenant and kingdom until his second coming. But what about the many other institutions and communities of this world? After rising from the dead Christ declared that "all authority in heaven and on earth has been given to me" (Matt. 28:18), and Paul explains that Christ has been seated at God's right hand "far above all rule and authority and power and dominion, and above every name that is named, not only in this age but also in the one to come" (Eph. 1:21). The Lord Jesus Christ rules all things. Yet it is only the church that can claim the privileges and blessings of the covenant of grace and the redemptive kingdom. Only at the second coming of Christ, at the sounding of the seventh trumpet, do the voices in heaven proclaim: "the kingdom of the world has become the kingdom of our Lord and of his Christ . . ." (Rev. 11:15). So how does Christ now rule the many institutions and communities of this world other than the church?

The answer is that he rules them through *the Noahic covenant*, for they are institutions and communities of the common kingdom. They operate according to the same basic principles and purposes as before Christ's first coming. What is different is that God now rules them through the incarnate Lord Jesus, the last Adam who has entered into the glory of the world-to-come. The common kingdom still exists and is very important for understanding the ongoing cultural life of this world, but its time is short, for the last Adam is coming again soon to bring this present world to its appointed end.

The New Testament does not say explicitly that God still rules the broader cultural life of this world through the Noahic covenant, but it does not have to. When he established the Noahic covenant, God said that it would continue "while the earth remains" (Gen. 8:22). Furthermore, Christ said nothing in the Gospels to indicate that his first coming meant to bring the institutions and communities of this world to an end. As we saw in Matthew, Christ taught that his ministry meant the end of the *Mosaic covenant*, because the coming of the kingdom of heaven and the establishment of the church brought the Mosaic covenant to fulfillment. But this does not mean the end of the Noahic covenant. Christians can still serve in the military and must still pay taxes. Believers today, as sojourners and exiles like Abraham and Daniel, live in *two kingdoms*. Only at Christ's second coming will the earth no longer endure and the Noahic covenant come to an end.

This section will first consider what the New Testament says about the common kingdom and Christians' involvement in it. Then I will offer some reflections on the proper Christian attitude toward the common kingdom as believers seek to be faithful sojourners and exiles whose true citizenship lies in Christ's heavenly kingdom, the world-to-come.

The Common Kingdom and the Institutions and Communities of This World

As observed in chapter 4, God promised two basic things in the Noahic covenant: preservation of the natural order (Gen. 8:21–22; 9:8–17) and the human social order (Gen. 9:1–7). Two institutions of the social order, family and state, come especially into view. Twice God commands the human race to "be fruitful and multiply" (9:1, 7), indicating the importance of the family for the common kingdom. He also ordains that wrongdoers should be punished justly by their fellow human beings (9:5–6), indicating the importance of a political and judicial system. In light of this, it is no surprise that the family and state are the two institutions of the common kingdom that receive special attention in the New Testament.

First, what does the New Testament say about the family? It does *not* say that Christ established marriage or the family. Christ did not have to do so because God established them at creation (Gen. 2:20–24) and has continued to bless them under the Noahic covenant (Gen. 9:1, 7). But though the New Testament does not create the family, it acknowledges its existence, confirms the authority structures within it, and speaks of how Christ and the church make special use of the family in bestowing saving blessing. The New Testament indicates that being married and having children are good things that most Christians will pursue at some point in their lives (e.g., 1 Cor. 7:2, 36–38; 1 Tim. 5:14), though remaining unmarried is an excellent way of life for some Christians (1 Cor. 7:6–8, 32–38). Mutual obligations and authority structures exist within the family. Members of the family should love one another, especially husbands toward wives (Eph. 5:25–33; Col. 3:19). Parents should instruct and discipline their children in a loving way (Eph. 6:4; Col. 3:21). Children should obey and honor their parents (Eph. 6:1–3; Col. 3:20) and husbands should exercise a loving authority with respect to their wives (Eph. 5:22–33; Col. 3:18–19; 1 Pet. 3:1–7).

Unlike the church, the family is a common institution that God has ordained for believers and unbelievers alike. The New Testament refers to unbelievers as being in married relationships and speaks as if this is an ordinary thing needing no explanation (e.g., Matt. 27:19). When people become Christians, their marital status does not change. Unmarried people continue to be unmarried after conversion, and married people continue to be married after conversion, even if their spouses remain unbelievers (1 Cor. 7:12–14). In other words, the existence of a marriage is independent of whether the spouses are Christians. That the family is part of the common kingdom is reinforced by the fact that it exists only temporarily. There will be no marriage in the world-to-come (Matt. 22:30; 1 Cor. 7:29–31; Rev. 18:23).

Christians nevertheless have some special responsibilities and privileges within their family relations. They should only marry other Christians (1 Cor. 7:39; 2 Cor. 6:14), even though a Christian married to an unbeliever is truly married. As Christian parents raise their children, they should strive to "bring them up in the discipline and instruction of the Lord" (Eph. 6:4). Children of believers are even regarded as members of the church and heirs of the kingdom due to the covenant promises given to Abraham and still applying to Christians today.[19] Furthermore, Christian spouses have the

---

[19]E.g., see Genesis 17:9–14; Mark 10:14; Luke 18:16; Acts 2:39; 1 Corinthians 7:14; Ephesians 6:1–4. Many Reformed works on the subject of infant baptism explain this point well. For some recent examples, see J. V. Fesko, *Word, Water, and Spirit: A Reformed Perspective on Baptism* (Grand Rapids: Reformation Heritage Books, 2010), chap. 14; Bryan Holstrom, *Infant Baptism and the Silence of the New Testament* (Greenville: Ambassador International, 2008), chaps. 4–5; and Daniel R. Hyde, *Jesus Loves the Little Children: Why We Baptize Children* (Grandville, MI: Reformed Fellowship, 2006), chap. 4.

privilege of perceiving their marriage relationships as a reflection of that profound and blessed relationship between Christ and his church (Eph. 5:25–32). Though a common institution, the family is highly honored in the church.

What does the New Testament say about the state? As with the family, the New Testament does *not* say that Christ established the state. Again, he did not have to, because God long ago, particularly in the Noahic covenant, ordained that there be institutions for doing justice in society (Gen. 4:15; 9:5–6). The Old Testament frequently acknowledges pagan kings as rulers with legitimate (though not unlimited) authority. The stories of Abraham and Daniel discussed in chapter 4 illustrate this. While the New Testament does not create the state, it acknowledges the authority of civil government and the magistrates who hold office. Jesus recognizes Caesar's right to levy taxes (Matt. 22:15–22), and Paul speaks of civil magistrates having "authority . . . from God," being divinely "instituted" and "appointed," and being "God's servant for your good." Magistrates "bear the sword" for dealing justice to the good and the wicked and should be accorded all proper respect, even by payment of taxes (Rom. 13:1–7; see also 1 Tim. 2:1–2; Titus 3:1; 1 Pet. 2:13–17).

Like the family, the state and its civil magistrates are legitimate regardless of whether magistrates and citizens are Christians, since they exist under the Noahic covenant as part of the common kingdom. The civil magistrates recognized by the New Testament were, after all, officers of the *Roman Empire.* No one would have mistaken the Roman government and Roman magistrates as "Christian." Americans and other people living in Western democracies often like to complain about their governments, but we should keep in mind that we have it far better under our own governments—however badly they often behave—than the early Christians had it under Rome. Furthermore, the New Testament never indicates that civil authorities have any responsibility to make the social or political order conform to the redemptive kingdom of heaven. What Christians are to expect from the state is simply the enforcement of justice so that they may lead a "peaceful and quiet life" (1 Tim. 2:2; see Rom. 13:3–4). This is precisely what we would expect from an institution of the common kingdom that exists under the Noahic covenant (see Gen. 9:5–6). In fact, something that Paul says in Romans 13:4 highlights how dangerous it is to associate the state with the redemptive kingdom rather than the common kingdom. The state is to "bear the sword" against the "wrongdoer" in order to bring justice. Jesus made it very clear in the Sermon on the Mount that the life of the kingdom of heaven here and now is to be nonviolent in response to wrongdoers: turn the other cheek. If the state wishes to operate according to the ways of the redemptive kingdom as revealed by Jesus then it must forsake the sword—the very thing that Paul says it must not do. When Paul says that the state should bear the sword he is saying, in essence, that the state belongs to the common kingdom under the Noahic covenant, not to the redemptive kingdom under the covenant of grace.

Thus Christians are to participate in the life of the family and the life of the state, though these institutions are not uniquely Christian. Under the Noahic covenant, family and state pertain to both believers and unbelievers, and the New Testament indicates that this holds true between the two comings of Christ. Living in families and living under the state are shared experiences among those who profess Christ and those who do not.

Though the New Testament gives special attention to the family and state as institutions of the common kingdom, family life and politics are not the only cultural activities in which Christians should engage. The New Testament, for example, speaks on many occasions about the responsibility of Christians to buy and sell and to work industriously in ordinary occupations (e.g., 1 Cor. 7:30; Eph. 4:28; 5:5–9; Col. 3:23; 1 Thess. 4:11; 2 Thess. 3:6–12). Christians remain Christians as they do these things, and these texts make clear that Christ is honored by our ordinary labor. But Paul also envisions this as activity that Christians do in common with unbelievers. He assumes, for example, that when Christians work hard with their hands they do so "before outsiders . . ." (1 Thess. 4:12; see vv. 11–12). The New Testament gives no indication that Christians should set up their own financial markets or establish networks of Christian businesses that deal only with each other. Running a business and doing ordinary work are activities of the common kingdom.

This discussion about matters such as daily occupations and political life—to be considered further in chapter 7—are summed up well in Paul's exhortations in 1 Corinthians 5. Paul urges the church to be a holy community and to follow disciplinary proceedings against those who do not repent of their sin. Because the church is the earthly manifestation of the kingdom of heaven, Paul demands that the church be set apart from the world, and he lays down a pattern for discipline that is nonviolent and seeks reconciliation and repentance (just as Jesus did in Matt. 18:15–20). But Paul also comments: "I wrote to you in my letter not to associate with sexually immoral people—not at all meaning the sexually immoral of this world, or the greedy and swindlers, or idolaters, since then you would need to go out of the world. But now I am writing to you not to associate with anyone who bears the name of brother if he is guilty of sexual immorality or greed, or is an idolater, reviler, drunkard, or swindler—not even to eat with such a one" (1 Cor. 5:9–11). Paul wants *the church* to be set apart and holy, but he does not want Christians "to go out of the world." In the world, as it continues to exist under the Noahic covenant, Paul expects that Christians will engage in activities such as work and politics in common with unbelievers.

A Christian Perspective on the Common Kingdom
Chapter 7 considers in detail the Christian's task in the broader world of human culture. For now, I offer a few reflections about the proper Christian attitude toward the common kingdom. The New Testament indicates that Christians should be involved in this kingdom and instills a basic perspective that should shape all of their cultural pursuits.

On several occasions the Old Testament encourages God's people to pursue their cultural activities with joy and satisfaction. Ecclesiastes, though warning about the vanity of life's pleasures when considered only on their own terms (1:2; 2:1–2), offers some good examples. "There is nothing better for a person than that he should eat and drink and find enjoyment in his toil. This also, I saw, is from the hand of God" (2:24). "Go, eat your bread in joy, and drink your wine with a merry heart, for God has already approved what you do. Let your garments be always white. Let not oil be lacking on your head. Enjoy life with the wife whom you love, all the days of your vain life that he has given you under the sun, because that is your portion in life and in your toil at which you toil under the sun" (9:7–9). Such instructions are an important part of the wisdom that God commends during our life "under the sun," which we as New Testament Christians are still experiencing. God continues to give us food and drink, spouses, gainful employment, and so many other things. These are parts of *God's* creation, and they are truly good and to be received with gratitude.

Yet it is interesting that we find so little in the New Testament that sounds like these verses in Ecclesiastes. Many recent books about Christianity and culture emphasize how good God's creation is, how much joy we should find in experiencing and exploring various areas of creation, and how central such work is to our Christian lives. These emphases can serve as a helpful corrective in response to certain Christian traditions that have tended to look at this world simply as evil and to find no inherent value in cultural activities (perhaps justifying them only insofar as they are necessary for feeding our families or providing opportunities for evangelism). It *is* correct to view cultural activities as gifts of God and as opportunities to please and glorify him. But the inherent goodness of cultural activities is not at all the emphasis of the New Testament. In comparison to many contemporary books that issue rousing calls to honor God in our studies, occupations, music, and other cultural activities, the New Testament is much more subdued and cautionary. We must continue to affirm with Ecclesiastes the goodness of cultural life, but should temper this affirmation with the perspective of the New Testament. I believe that this New Testament perspective can be helpfully summarized in three points.

First, Christians should pursue cultural activities not with a spirit of triumph and conquest over their neighbors but with a spirit of love and service toward them. Far too often Christian writers and leaders imbue their audience with a drive to take over—to take over politics, education, the courts, and whatever else (or maybe it is put in more palatable terms, such as taking *back* instead of taking *over*, as if Christians are the rightful owners of everything and are simply reclaiming what is already theirs). The New Testament does call us "more than conquerors through him who loved us" (Rom. 8:37), and on the day of Christ's return we will share in his visible triumph over his enemies (e.g., 2 Thess. 1:5–10). But until then God calls us to be involved in activities such as education and politics not in order to trounce *opponents* but to serve *neighbors*. "You have heard that it was said, 'You shall love your neighbor and hate your enemy.' But I say to you, Love your enemies and pray for those who persecute you" (Matt. 5:43–44). The apparent enemy *is* our neighbor (Luke 10:25–37). It is all too easy to demonize those with whom we disagree and to seek to vilify them for their sins in order to gain tactical advantage—even though their conduct often outshines our own in many areas of life, and though, if we do avoid their sins, we do so only by the unmerited grace of God. We have been justified in Christ precisely so that we may love and serve our neighbor, for this is the fulfillment of the law (Rom. 13:8–10; Gal. 5:13–14). The New Testament constantly calls us to gentleness, meekness, patience, and humility (e.g., Matt. 5:5; Gal. 5:22–23; Eph. 4:2). If only we were as eager to deal with our own many sins as we are to expose the sins of others whom we regard as our cultural opponents—if only we would learn to take the log out of our own eyes before seeing the speck in another's eye (Matt. 7:1–5). The way of love and service in all areas of culture, not the way of vilification and conquest, is the proper Christian attitude.

Perhaps we could learn a little lesson from Genesis 26:14–31, during Isaac's days of sojourning. Isaac, like his father Abraham, but under different circumstances, made a covenant with the pagan king Abimelech. The Philistines originally sent Isaac away because he was too powerful. And he went. Then the Philistines quarreled with him about wells that *Abraham* had dug and that *Isaac himself* had reopened. Isaac moved on. Finally the Philistines came to him and asked to make a covenant. He agreed. Isaac's attitude was not one of overcoming the enemy or pressing his rights, but living in peace with all as far as he could (see also Rom. 12:18).

Second, the New Testament calls us to critical engagement with human culture. The Christian attitude of love and service toward *neighbors*, which shuns the vilification and humiliation of *enemies*, does not at all mean that we should think uncritically about the cultural life around us. As in the days of Abraham and the Babylonian exile, cultural commonality is never meant to eliminate the spiritual antithesis. Even while we seek to treat all people with charity and generosity, we must remain vigilant and perceptive about the many ways that sin has corrupted human culture in this fallen world. In the face of the decay and rebellion at work around us Paul exhorts: "Do not be conformed to this world, but be transformed by the renewal of your mind, that by testing you may discern what is the will of God, what is good and acceptable and perfect" (Rom. 12:2). Elsewhere Paul states: "We destroy arguments and every lofty opinion raised against the knowledge of God, and take every thought captive to obey Christ" (2 Cor. 10:5). It is also important to remember what Paul says immediately before this: "For though we walk in the flesh, we are not waging war according to the flesh. For the weapons of our warfare are not of the flesh but have divine power to destroy strongholds" (10:3–4). Paul calls Christians to think rightly about all sorts of things, to engage critically the rebellious thoughts of this world, and to be on guard against the "philosophy and empty deceit" that seeks to take *us* "captive" (see Col. 2:8). Yet we do so not with the weapons of the flesh, such as military weapons, political tactics, or media propaganda. God summons us to critical thinking and nonconformity, even while we engage in cultural tasks alongside unbelievers and strive to serve them in humility and meekness. Not an easy task!

Third and finally, the New Testament calls us to engage in cultural activities with a deep sense of detachment from this world and of longing for our true home in the world-to-come. Our cultural engagement is important, but it is not *that* important. In comparison to "the glory that is to be revealed to us" (Rom. 8:18) our cultural labors—with their temporary successes and failures, their joys and disappointments—can only seem fleeting. What are the treasures of this life in comparison with the "treasures of heaven" (Matt. 6:20; see vv. 19–20) and with the life "which is truly life" (1 Tim. 6:19)? The social position that we occupy is not crucial for our standing before Christ (1 Cor. 7:17–24). Even honorable activities of human culture such as marriage and commerce are of modest importance in relation to eternity: "The appointed time has grown very short. From now on, let those who have wives live as though they had none, and those who mourn as though they were not mourning, and those who rejoice as though they were not rejoicing, and those who buy as though they had no goods, and those who deal with the world as though they had no dealings with it. For the present form of this world is passing away" (1 Cor. 7:29–31). We set our minds on things above, not on things on earth because our *life* is "hidden with God in Christ" (Col. 3:3; see vv. 2–3), because "our citizenship is in heaven . . ." (Phil. 3:20; see vv. 19–20). We seek not the success and glory of the present age, but instead we must "go to him [Jesus] outside the camp and bear the reproach he endured. For here we have no lasting city, but we seek the city that is to come" (Heb. 13:13–14). The grace of God trains us not for earthly conquest but trains us "to renounce ungodliness and worldly passions, and to live self-controlled, upright, and godly lives in the present age, waiting for our blessed hope, the appearing of the glory of our great God and Savior Jesus Christ" (Titus 2:12–13).

This sense of detachment from the present world and longing for the world-to-come is the attitude that the New Testament impresses upon Christians. It is the attitude appropriate for sojourners and exiles. Abraham "was looking forward to the city that has foundations, whose designer and builder is God" (Heb. 11:10). He and the saints of old "acknowledged that they were strangers and exiles on the earth," "seeking a homeland," desiring "a better country, that is, a heavenly one. Therefore God is not ashamed to be called their God, for he has prepared for them a city" (Heb. 11:14–16). As we saw at the end of the previous chapter, Daniel diligently served his (pagan) neighbors without lording it over them, he maintained a critical eye and refused to participate in Babylonian customs that violated God's law, and most of all he longed to return to Jerusalem at the end of the seventy-year exile. No wonder Peter uses the terms *sojourner* and *exile* to describe the state of Christians as they seek to live godly cultural lives at the end of the ages.

Conclusion

We have seen in this chapter that the age between Christ's ascension and his second coming is an age in which Christians are called to live as members of two kingdoms. Both the common kingdom and the redemptive kingdom exist by God's ordination and under his moral government, but God rules them in different ways and for different purposes. In both kingdoms Christians offer loving service to God and neighbor. As they live in two kingdoms, however, Christians must remember that only one of these kingdoms is destined to endure. They live in the common kingdom as sojourners and exiles, waiting eagerly for Christ, the last Adam, to return and to usher in his redemptive kingdom in the fullness of its glory.

Some important questions remain before us. What are the implications for how the church should operate, and how should Christians understand their place within it? How should Christians, as sojourners and exiles, conduct themselves as students, as workers, or as citizens in the midst of the institutions and activities of the common kingdom? Is there a Christian view—a two-kingdoms vision—of learning, vocation, and politics? In part 3 I reflect upon these sorts of concrete questions by building on the biblical and theological foundations explored in these previous chapters.

PART THREE

CHRISTIAN LIFE
IN THE TWO KINGDOMS

Part 2 traced the development of the two kingdoms through the biblical story. The common kingdom was formally established in the covenant with Noah in Genesis 8:20–9:17, and the redemptive kingdom was formally established in the covenant with Abraham in Genesis 15 and 17. In the Old Testament, Abraham, Isaac, and Jacob and later the exiles in Babylon were called to live in these two kingdoms, being radically distinguished from the world in their faith, worship, and eschatological hope while being called to live in common with the world in a variety of cultural pursuits. The New Testament calls Christians *sojourners* and *exiles* and hence casts our eyes back to the days of Abraham and the Babylonian captivity in order to instruct us how to live in this present age as we wait for our Lord, the last Adam, to return and usher in the world-to-come. Until then we seek to live obedient lives to God in every area of life, recognizing that God rules both of these kingdoms and also that he rules them in different ways.

Part 2 considered these matters rather generally. But what does the Christian life in these two kingdoms look like more particularly? It would be impossible in a short book like this to give a comprehensive answer to that question, but part 3 attempts to add some flesh to the skeleton provided in part 2. Chapters 6 and 7 examine each of the two kingdoms respectively. Chapter 6 considers the church as the earthly manifestation of the kingdom of heaven. We will explore the church's nature and characteristics as well as the importance and distinctiveness of the Christian life within the church. I argue that the church should be central to the believer's Christian life and that the church is a wonderful and mysterious community that is radically different from the communities and institutions of the common kingdom. Without understanding the Christian's calling within the church it is very difficult to understand how the Christian should perform his various cultural tasks in the broader world. Chapter 6, therefore, should prepare us for chapter 7, which explores the Christian's responsibilities within the communities and institutions of the common kingdom. By focusing on three particularly controversial and important areas of cultural life in chapter 7—education, vocation, and politics—I hope to provide a general vision for how Christians may pursue obedience to their Lord in all of their common cultural activities.

The Church

CHAPTER 5 PRESENTED the church of Jesus Christ as a strange and wonderful thing. Built by Christ and united to him by faith, the church is the one and only earthly institution today that can claim the promises of the Abrahamic covenant of grace and can identify itself with the redemptive kingdom, the kingdom of heaven proclaimed by Christ. Though it resembles other earthly institutions in some outward ways, it is *not* just one earthly institution out of many. While God rules and preserves every other institution through the Noahic covenant, he bestows salvation on the church alone through the Abrahamic covenant of grace. All other institutions serve good and honorable purposes at present, but they await termination at the day of Christ's return. The church, in contrast, awaits Christ's return as a day of consummation, when as the bride of Christ she will take her place at the wedding banquet of the Lamb (see Eph. 5:22–32; Rev. 19:9–10).

Books about Christianity and culture often spend much time speaking about cultural activities such as education, vocation, and politics but say little about the church. Undoubtedly the authors of these books would profess that the church is important. But many of them seem to treat the church as of secondary importance for the Christian life and the various activities of human culture as where Christianity is *really* lived. In this book I defend the opposite position. The church is primary for the Christian life. Every other institution—the family, the school, the business corporation, the state—is secondary in the practice of the Christian religion. The church is where the chief action of the Christian life takes place. If we do not understand that fact, then we will also fail to understand secondary aspects of our Christian life, such as studying, working, and voting.

Accordingly, we will explore the Christian's calling within the church here in chapter 6 and then move on to consider the Christian's calling in the broader culture in chapter 7. In chapter 6 I first address the perhaps surprising and seemingly outrageous claim that the church is of primary importance for the Christian life. Then I reflect upon some of the distinctive aspects of the church's ethic. In all sorts of ways the church's way of life is to be different—in some ways radically different—from the various ethics of the institutions of the common kingdom. In the last sections of the chapter I discuss two attributes of the church, its *spirituality* and its *ministerial authority*. These attributes are crucial for understanding its nature and the ethic by which it conducts itself, yet they are so often misunderstood or entirely unacknowledged. These categories help to remind the church to do the things it is supposed to do—and not to do things that it should not.

The Centrality of the Church for the Christian Life

What exactly are you doing when you go to church on Sundays? If you had to analogize going to church with something in everyday life, what would that analogy be? One popular analogy is that going to church is like stopping at a gas station. Church is a place where we stop to fill up our tanks after a tiring and stressful week and thus get recharged for the week ahead. Another analogy compares going to church to a huddle in a football game. Church is the gathering of all the team's players so that they can regroup, encourage each other, and prepare for separating again and facing the opponent through the coming week. Are these effective analogies for understanding the church?

I suggest that these analogies are radically insufficient and misleading. Perhaps most obviously, these analogies portray going to church as a human-centered event. Going to church is not primarily about me or even about us, but about God. I go to church not first of all to benefit myself (though that is a very important secondary effect) but to worship the Lord. A second deficiency in these analogies is that they place the real action of the Christian life somewhere other than in the gathering of God's people for worship. Athletes do not play football in order to huddle and fans do not attend games in order to watch the huddles—what athletes and fans really care about are the plays executed when the ball is snapped. People do not go on road trips in order to stop for gas—drivers and passengers set out to enjoy the scenery and to arrive at their destination. Huddles and gas stations are means to an end. The life and ministry of the church are *not* means to an end. They do not exist to recharge our batteries or to give us a strategy for facing the week ahead. The church's worship and fellowship are ends in themselves. Nothing that we do in this world is more important than participating in these activities. Participation in the life of the church, not participation in the cultural activities of the broader world, is central for the Christian life. A few considerations may help to illumine this claim.

The Church as the Redemptive Kingdom

The first consideration is a general one that recalls a major theme of chapter 5: the church is the only earthly institution that can identify itself with the redemptive kingdom. To have fellowship with the church is to have fellowship with the kingdom of heaven that Jesus proclaimed. The Christian's "life" is in heaven, hidden with Christ in God (Col. 3:1–4), and the Christian's true "citizenship" is in heaven, from where Christ will return again (Phil. 3:20–21). If the life of the world-to-come defines who we really and truly are, then the earthly community that opens the gates to this kingdom and bestows its fellowship upon us has pride of place over those that do not. The family, the state, the school, and the workplace are all honorable and useful communities, and we should strive to participate in them in ways worthy of our heavenly citizenship. But none of them is the kingdom of heaven on earth. The church ought to be central to the Christian life because the church is the only earthly community that manifests the redemptive kingdom and grants us the fellowship of our true home, the world-to-come.

Worship

Second, the church ought to be central to the Christian life because the church is the special community that renders *worship* to God. There are many things that we do not know about our future lives in heaven. What sorts of artistic or scientific tasks we might have in the New Jerusalem is a mystery. But what we do know without any doubt is that the world-to-come will be a place saturated with worship. "Then I saw another sign in heaven. . . . I saw what appeared to be a sea of glass mingled with fire—and also those who had conquered the beast and its image and the number of its name, standing beside the sea of glass with harps of God in their hands. And they sing the song of Moses, the servant of God, and the song of the Lamb, saying, 'Great and amazing are your deeds, O Lord God the Almighty! Just and true are your ways, O King of the nations! Who will not fear, O Lord, and glorify your name? For you alone are holy. All nations will come and worship you, for your righteous acts have been revealed'" (Rev. 15:1–4). "No longer will there be anything accursed, but the throne of God and of the Lamb will be in it, and his servants will worship him" (Rev. 22:3). Since our fellowship with the life of heaven is central to the Christian life, and since heaven is a realm of worship above all else, then our present-day worship must be central to our Christian life. This again points us to the church, for the church is first and foremost a community of worship.

The claim that the church is primarily a community of worship could be easily misunderstood. Some people today, with pious intentions, assert that all of life should be worship to God. It is true, of course, that God calls us to glorify him in all that we do (1 Cor. 10:31), and he is pleased when we undertake any task righteously, but Scripture also speaks of a special activity that is more properly deemed "worship." Such worship consists essentially in God's speaking to us (through the reading and preaching of his Word and the administration of sacraments as his visible word) and his people speaking back to him (through prayer and song). Such worship is an activity of the redemptive kingdom alone. Believers share a variety of cultural activities with unbelievers in the common kingdom, but worship has never been one of them. The universal Noahic covenant of Genesis 9 commanded nothing about worship.[1] In contrast, in the Abrahamic covenant of grace, Abraham was *distinguished* from the world by the sacramental act of circumcision and his building altars to the Lord (Gen. 12:7–8; 17:9–14). God also distinguished Old Testament Israel from the world when he gave them prophets and priests to minister his word and established the temple and sacrificial system for their acts of worship. In the exile Daniel and his friends were distinguished from the Babylonians by refusing to join in their pagan worship and insisting that worship belongs to the true God alone (Dan. 3:1–30; 6:1–24). So too in the New Testament, present-day sojourners and exiles, in distinction from the world, have been made a royal priesthood to offer "spiritual sacrifices" to God and to "proclaim the excellencies of him who called you out of darkness into his marvelous light" (1 Pet. 2:5, 9; see vv. 4–11). Many non-Christians are very religious, of course. But however earnest, their worship is ultimately false and useless. Only those who have been justified through Christ are adopted as God's children and can call on him as "our Father" (e.g., Matt. 6:9–13; Rom. 8:1–17; Gal. 3:26–4:7). Only they, by God's grace alone, can respond to God's summons with faith and offer worship as a foretaste of that heavenly worship in the world-to-come.

As an activity of the redemptive kingdom, worship is an activity of the church. Believers, as individuals and families, are obliged to offer private worship to God, since Scripture exhorts us to meditate on God's word day and night (Ps. 1:2) and to pray without ceasing (1 Thess. 5:17). Scripture's special concern, however, is with *corpo-*

---

[1]See note 2 in chapter 4 concerning Noah's altar-building in Genesis 8:20.

rate worship, in the gathered assembly of the saints. For example, Paul gives distinct instructions for corporate worship that do not apply in other contexts (1 Cor. 11:33–34; 14:26–40). Hebrews warns believers about "neglecting to meet together" (Heb. 10:25) and later commands "us" to worship God "with reverence and awe," since our worship brings us into fellowship with the worship of the heavenly Jerusalem (Heb. 12:28; see vv. 18–29). Why is it not enough to worship privately? For one thing, heavenly worship is a corporate activity (e.g., Heb. 12:22–23; Rev. 19:1–8), and thus corporate worship on earth is the richest foretaste of worship in heaven. Furthermore, God has ordained corporate worship as the special occasion for bestowing the word and sacraments upon his people, as "means of grace" that build them up unto everlasting life. Reading Scripture privately is good, but hearing it preached by a faithful minister of the gospel is even better. The church is to ordain gifted and godly men for this labor of ministering the word (1 Tim. 3:1–7; 2 Tim. 2:2; Titus 1:5–9) and this ministry works faith (Rom. 10:14–17) and protects the flock against false teaching (Acts 20:26–32; 2 Tim. 4:1–5). The New Testament also indicates that the Lord's Supper is to be celebrated corporately in the church (1 Cor. 11:17–34). This holy Supper is a "participation in the blood of Christ [and] . . . the body of Christ" (1 Cor. 10:16), a foretaste of the wedding banquet in the world-to-come (Matt. 22:1–14; Rev. 19:6–10). Since the church's corporate worship is where all of this takes place, such worship is central for the Christian life.

The Lord's Day

The observance of Sunday as the Lord's Day also highlights the centrality of the church for the Christian life. Throughout history many Christians have acknowledged Sunday as a holy day, set apart from the other days of the week as a day of worship and of rest from ordinary cultural activities. Recent generations have increasingly neglected this practice, even in Christian traditions that historically have prized Lord's Day observance. Many churches that still take corporate worship seriously devote only a short period on Sunday morning to worship and Christian fellowship and leave the rest of the day free for work, shopping, or sports. This is a tragic development. It is not as if observing the Lord's Day leaves Christians little time for common cultural activities—even believers who dedicate all of Sunday to worship and Christian fellowship still have six of the seven days of the week to pursue other things. Yet in the present day our common cultural activities increasingly tend to encroach into Sunday as well, so that the majority of this day also becomes dedicated to the activities of the common kingdom.

There are good biblical reasons to resist this tendency and to devote the whole of Sunday to the affairs of the redemptive kingdom, and thus primarily to the life of the church.[2] Lord's Day observance is in fact a brilliant way to be counter-cultural and to offer testimony to a world that claims its own all-consuming importance. By keeping the Lord's Day holy we testify that we are willing to set aside our cultural labors for a day and to suffer whatever harmful consequences that may bring for advancement in this world, because we belong to another kingdom that is of much greater importance and is the source of our true hope and confidence.

Understanding the biblical teaching on observance of the Lord's Day requires beginning in the Old Testament, though certainly not ending there. As we saw in chapter 2, God himself established the sabbatical pattern of working six days and resting one day (Gen. 1:1–2:3). We also saw that the first Adam, as God's image-bearer, was commissioned to follow his maker's pattern by working in this world toward the goal of resting in the world-to-come. Bearing God's image is intimately related to observing a sabbatical pattern of work and rest. In the first explicit biblical command for God's people to observe a weekly Sabbath (Ex. 20:8, 11), the text appeals back to creation and calls people to image God the Creator: "Remember the Sabbath day, to keep it holy. . . . For in six days the LORD made heaven and earth. . . ." One of the key purposes of the Old Testament Sabbath, therefore, was to remind Israel of God's original work and of the basic human obligation to image God by obediently working in this world and attaining God's blessing as a result.

---

[2] I would also adhere to the traditional idea that cultural works of necessity and mercy are permitted, and even required, on the Lord's Day.

In the bigger picture considered in chapters 4–5, the Mosaic covenant served to teach God's people that they could never fulfill this obligation and that they must look instead to a free gift of grace through a coming Messiah. One way in which the Old Testament pointed them to the coming of Christ was by giving them a second kind of Sabbath that was different from the ordinary weekly Sabbaths. For a couple of special occasions God gave Israel the equivalent of an *eighth day* rest—or, a rest on the *first day* of the week (see Lev. 23:15–16, 21; 25:8–12; see vv. 1–12). Leviticus 23 teaches about the Feast of Weeks and commands a rest on the fiftieth day (a Sunday), following seven cycles of seven-day weeks. Leviticus 25 speaks about a Sabbath year, the Year of Jubilee, a time when people were released from their debts and restored to their inheritance. This Year of Jubilee took place on the *fiftieth* year, the year after "seven times seven years," that is, seven squared, the perfect number of ordinary cycles of years. Liberty was to be proclaimed throughout the land (25:8, 10). This was the year for showcasing the grace of God that conquers all evil. This practice of celebrating a Sabbath on the fiftieth day/year must have been wonderful for the Old Testament Israelites, but a little confusing nonetheless. The ordinary weekly Sabbath was about working first and only then taking a rest. But here they were instructed to rest *at the beginning* of the cycle of time, *before* the period for work.

What was the meaning of this different kind of Old Testament Sabbath? It pointed ahead to the resurrection of the Lord Jesus Christ. During his earthly ministry Jesus announced on a Sabbath day (Saturday) the fulfillment of the proclamation of liberty, "the year of the Lord's favor" (Luke 4:19; see vv. 16–21). Jesus pointed Israel to himself as the one who brings the true and ultimate Jubilee for his people. How exactly did he bring the final and greatest liberty to them, a liberty that far surpasses a (temporary) return to an earthly plot of land? He did it through the resurrection. Jesus rose "after the Sabbath" (Matt. 28:1; Mark 16:1), on the "first day of the week" (Luke 24:1; John 20:1)—Sunday. The timing is truly amazing. The day that Jesus lay dead in the tomb turned out to be the last Sabbath of the Old Testament era (for after his resurrection the old covenant was no more). Remember that the Old Testament Year of Jubilee had occurred on the fiftieth year—that is, the year immediately after the "perfect" number of Sabbath years ($7 \times 7 = 49$). And thus Jesus rose from the dead on the day immediately after the number of Old Testament seventh-day Sabbaths had reached their complete and perfect number! His resurrection was the true Year of Jubilee. The weekly Old Testament Sabbath had looked back to God's work of creation (Ex. 20:8–11) and reminded God's people of the first Adam's original obligation to work perfectly in this world and then to attain his rest. The resurrection now announces that Jesus, as the last Adam, has completed the task of the first Adam and has attained his reward of rest in the world-to-come.

This means true and perfect liberty for God's people. We need not try to be a bunch of second Adams, performing Adam's cultural labors in order to attain the world-to-come. Jesus accomplished Adam's task once and for all, and did it for us. Thus we are justified not by the works of our hands but by faith alone in the perfect work of the resurrected Christ. This is why it is a terrible thing for Christians to continue to observe a seventh day Sabbath. No longer do we work first and then rest.[3]

What we do instead is rest first, and only then take up our work. Sunday—the first day of the week, the day of resurrection—became the day on which Christ met with his disciples (John 20:19, 26) and on which the church gathered for its worship (Acts 20:7; 1 Cor. 16:1–2). As the seventh-day Sabbath of the Old Testament testified that the task assigned to the first Adam remained uncompleted, so the first-day Sabbath of the New Testament testifies that the last Adam has fulfilled it. By resting first and then working, the Christian doctrine of salvation is portrayed in live action. God first justifies us by uniting us to his resurrected Son in heaven apart from any work of our own, and then he calls us to work obediently in this world, not to earn our rest but to express our gratitude that the rest has already

---

[3]For a helpful short piece that explains the Sabbath in a way similar to my presentation, see Brenton C. Ferry, "The Age of Jubilee: A Redemptive-Historical Case for the Christian Sabbath," *New Horizons* (April 2009): 8–9. In the same issue see another helpful essay on the topic: John R. Muether, "The Sabbath: Plausibility for Presbyterian Pilgrims," *New Horizons* (April 2009): 3–5.

been earned by the work of another. We are still image-bearers of God, thus we are still Sabbath-keepers by nature. But we no longer bear the image after the pattern of the first Adam but after the pattern of Christ, the last Adam (1 Cor. 15:47–49; Rom. 8:29). We keep the Sabbath in a way that shows that the true rest has already been attained. We rest by free grace, and only then do we work.

Contrary to popular perception, observing Sunday as the Lord's Day should not be a legalistic rule about what we cannot do, but a glorious and refreshing practice in which we focus our attention fully on the things that are most important, the things of the redemptive kingdom of heaven. By laying aside our ordinary cultural activities and devoting ourselves to worship and Christian fellowship—as individual Christians and especially as the church—we receive a foretaste of the life of the heavenly city that we long to enter.[4] What a delight this should be for Christians: a day to set aside fleeting cultural endeavors without feeling any guilt for being lazy and to revel in the heavenly things, our true treasure (Matt. 6:19–21). Will the world look at us as unproductive and silly? Probably, but what a glorious witness the church offers when it observes the Lord's Day. We provide the world with a living picture of our justification and testify that though we willingly work and play in common with them for six days, there is one day in which we refrain from common activities so that we can gather as a holy people unto Christ (and we hold out the invitation to all that they might join us in this rest by trusting Christ and calling upon his name). Perhaps we will fall behind our earthly competitors if we devote only six days a week to our cultural endeavors. But if we must do so for the sake of Christ and his heavenly kingdom, should that not be a privilege?

As we come to the end of this first section of the chapter, therefore, the first practical implication that we should draw from the

---

[4]John Murray writes: "The sabbath institution in all its aspects and application has this prospective reference; the whole movement of redemption will find its finale in the Sabbath rest that remains. The weekly Sabbath is the promise, token, and foretaste of the consummated rest; it is also the earnest. The biblical philosophy of the Sabbath is such that to deny its perpetuity is to deprive the movement of redemption of one of its most precious strands." See "The Sabbath Institution," in *Collected Writings of John Murray*, vol. 1, *The Claims of Truth* (Edinburgh: Banner of Truth, 1976), 216.

two-kingdoms doctrine is that it places the church front and center in the Christian life. Cultural work is honorable, but we must approach it in a way that respects the priority of corporate worship and the celebration of the Lord's Day. The church is the redemptive kingdom here on earth, and where the church is not our first love we are doomed to take an unhealthy perspective on the cultural activities of the common kingdom.

The Church's Distinctive Ethic

What does life look like within this church that stands at the center of the Christian life? How should Christians, in their various roles within her, conduct themselves toward God and in interaction with one another and the world? The rest of the chapter develops a basic answer to this question from the perspective of a biblical two-kingdoms doctrine. In this section I consider three noteworthy aspects of the church's ethic that mark it out as radically distinct from the institutions of the common kingdom (even at their best): it exhibits forgiveness that transcends justice, it exhibits generosity that transcends scarcity, and it pursues evangelism that spurns violence.

Forgiveness That Transcends Justice

Pursuing justice is a central task of the *common* kingdom, as the Noahic covenant teaches (Gen. 9:6). The New Testament makes clear that God appoints civil magistrates to proclaim judgment (Rom. 13:1–7). Proportionate justice is the ideal: "Whoever *sheds the blood* of man, by man *shall his blood be shed*" (Gen. 9:6), a principle commonly summarized as "eye for eye, tooth for tooth" (Ex. 21:23–25; Lev. 24:18–21; Deut. 19:21), whether enforced literally or not. As discussed in chapter 5, Jesus announced that this principle of justice is not to apply in the kingdom of heaven (Matt. 5:38–42). Instead an ethic of forgiveness and reconciliation should characterize the citizens of his kingdom, an ethic that portrays the gospel itself.

This ethic should characterize the church. Matthew 18:15–20 and 1 Corinthians 5 teach that the church must administer discipline in order to deal with its members who refuse to repent of sin (a responsibility widely ignored in many churches today). But church discipline should look exceedingly different from civil justice in the state. The necessity of church discipline is prompted by serious sin against God and neighbor (see Matt. 18:15; 1 Cor. 5:1). Yet Scripture never speaks of *enforcing justice* against the wrongdoer as the goal of church discipline. The goal is *restoration* (Matt. 18:15; 1 Cor. 5:5; 2 Cor. 2:7–10; Gal. 6:1). Matthew 18:15–17 describes four steps of church discipline: speaking to the wrongdoer privately, speaking to him with one or two others, the church as a whole speaking to him, and finally the act of excommunication—"let him be to you as a Gentile and a tax collector." At any step along the way the process comes to an abrupt end if the sinner repents: "if he listens to you, you have gained your brother." This is crucial to notice. In an ordinary civil lawsuit it is irrelevant whether an accused person repents. If he committed the crime, he should pay the penalty, whether he feels remorse or not. This is the demand of justice. But in the church it would be a travesty to continue the disciplinary process after repentance, out of desire to give the sinner his due. All citizens of Christ's heavenly kingdom rejoice that God has *not* given them their due, but like a shepherd sought them out when they wandered and forgave their debts like a merciful king (Matt. 18:12–14, 21–35). Church discipline aims to forgive, reconcile, and restore, not to enforce justice.

Therefore there are no criminal records in the church. No one who repents is blacklisted and no one is on probation, no matter how many civil crimes he has committed. A person might be prosecuted and convicted of a crime for which he stands perfectly forgiven in the eyes of Christ and his church. This does not mean, for example, that a repentant child-abuser should immediately be given church nursery duty like anyone else, for pastors, elders, and repentant sinners themselves ought to exercise wisdom about putting people in positions that may inflame temptation or give reason for scandal. But no one should exist in the church with the label "pedophile" or any other label. In contrast to the just and often permanent judgments of this world, what a beautiful haven of forgiveness the church should be.

Generosity That Transcends Scarcity

A second characteristic of the church's distinctive ethic is its generosity that transcends scarcity. Anyone who has studied economics—the economics of the common kingdom—has learned the fundamental principle of scarcity. Though worldly wealth is not exactly a fixed quantity that creates a zero-sum game (there is much more worldly wealth now than there was a thousand years ago), there is truly only so much to go around. A certain sum of money will only satisfy a certain number of needs or desires. A piece of property cannot be enjoyed by everyone. Worldly economics therefore explores the hard choices that people (and businesses and governments) have to make about how to use their inevitably limited resources. Individuals and institutions of the common kingdom may be full of good intentions, but they are constrained by an ethic of scarcity. In contrast, the New Testament reveals that an ethic of scarcity does not constrain the church. From a certain perspective it is true that churches set budgets based on expected giving and cannot cut checks to missionaries or the poor beyond the balance in their bank accounts. But as illuminating as worldly economics is for the commerce of the common kingdom, it can make little sense of the church's giving and receiving as described in Scripture.

In the redemptive kingdom the impoverished widow who gives two copper coins contributes more than all the offerings of the rich combined (Mark 12:41–44). This is not the way that the United States Department of the Treasury would (or should) view things. In the church "extreme poverty" overflows into a "wealth of generosity" that turns out to be an "abundance" that richly supplies the needs of others (2 Cor. 8:2, 14). It seems almost irrational when analyzed in earthly terms. In the common kingdom something does not come from nothing, but that seems to be exactly what happens in the church. Christians cheerfully desire to give "beyond their means" (8:3; see 9:7), and rather than rebuking them as fiscally irresponsible Paul actually praises them, for the Lord loves it.

The explanation lies not in a complex theory worthy of a Nobel Prize economist, but in the mysterious, wonderful, economics-defying work of God. He "is able to make all grace abound to you, so that having all sufficiency in all things at all times, you may abound in every good work" (2 Cor. 9:8). When the impoverished give generously God makes them "enriched" in the experience (9:11). In part this is about money, but only in part. This seemingly irresponsible generosity makes everyone spiritually richer in ways that economics cannot calculate: "For the ministry of this service is not only supplying the needs of the saints but is also overflowing in many thanksgivings to God. By their approval of this service, they will glorify God because of your submission flowing from your confession of the gospel of Christ, and the generosity of your contribution for them and for all others, while they long for you and pray for you, because of the surpassing grace of God upon you" (9:12–14). The God who owns the cattle on a thousand hills (Ps. 50:10) and who gives grace "to each one of us according to the measure of Christ's gift" (Eph. 4:7) can easily defy ordinary laws of economics. He can and does ensure that in the church those who give generously (of money, time, hospitality, prayer) do not thereby have less but somehow gain more in return. In light of this we can see why holding goods in common in the early church (Acts 4:32–37) could make sense, though it has never worked in any worldly attempt to create a communist utopia.

In the church there are no winners and losers, but every act of love is mutually enriching in Christ's economics—an economics built not on the principle of scarcity but on the principle of extravagant abundance. As the church defies the constraints of the common kingdom's justice so it also defies the constraints of its economics. Here is one important reason why the gospel is good news for the poor.

Evangelism That Spurns Violence
A third characteristic of the church that highlights its distinctive ethic is its evangelism that spurns violence. At the core of its being, the church is a missionary body. In the very first New Testament reference to "the church," the Lord Jesus entrusted the church with the "keys of the kingdom of heaven" (Matt. 16:18–19). The church is to be the gateway for entering the kingdom, and its servants are to go "to the main roads and invite to the wedding feast as many

as you find . . . both bad and good . . ." (Matt. 22:9–10). After his resurrection, in the Great Commission, Christ set the church on its course by commanding his disciples to "make disciples of all nations, baptizing them in the name of the Father and of the Son and of the Holy Spirit, teaching them to observe all that I have commanded you . . ." (Matt. 28:19–20). At this time he commissioned these apostles to be his witnesses "in Jerusalem and in all Judea and Samaria, and to the end of the earth" (Acts 1:8), a task fulfilled through the book of Acts, which ends in Rome, the capital of the world. Paul described their task: "we are ambassadors for Christ, God making his appeal through us. We implore you on behalf of Christ, be reconciled to God" (2 Cor. 5:20). Though Paul and the apostles had a unique task as eyewitnesses of the resurrected Christ, when they completed their ministry the church's evangelistic task had only just begun. Paul instructed Timothy, one of the ordinary pastors who would continue the task of ministering the Word, to devote himself "to the public reading of Scripture, to exhortation, to teaching" (1 Tim. 4:13) and thereby to "do the work of an evangelist" (2 Tim. 4:5). All ordinary Christians can also contribute to this evangelistic work in an informal way (1 Pet. 3:15).

This missionary task distinguishes the ethic of the church from the ethic of common kingdom institutions. Any earthly society that sees its task as evangelistic in nature has radically transgressed its proper boundaries. A Nazi regime that seeks to make the whole world German—or any American regime that seeks to make the whole world American, for that matter—is a frightening thing. No civil government could accomplish such a goal except by trampling other civil governments through unjust warfare. No particular culture could dominate the world except by a cultural imperialism that fails to respect the creativity of image-bearing human beings in other cultures. In contrast, the church rightly calls every person in this world to itself and invites them to forsake every other ultimate allegiance for the sake of Christ's kingdom. Yet it does so without violence and without any injustice. It forsakes "the weapons . . . of the flesh" (2 Cor. 10:4) and simply wins people to faith and salvation "through the folly of what we preach" (1 Cor. 1:21; see Rom.

10:14–17). This nonviolent missionary task not only sets the church apart from the institutions of the common kingdom but also from other world religions such as Judaism and Islam. Contemporary Judaism is essentially a nonproselytizing religion, content to let Judaism be for Jews while Gentiles relate to God in other ways. Islam is a proselytizing religion, but it seeks the aid of the sword to achieve and defend its claims. Islam's cultural claims are in fact all-encompassing, for it has no true doctrine of a distinction between mosque and state or any other cultural institution. Unlike Judaism, Christianity calls every individual in the world to itself. Unlike Islam, Christianity does so (or at least *should* do so) without pursuing violence or a broader social revolution.

The Spirituality of the Church

This chapter has already made some important claims about the church as the redemptive kingdom and about how Christians should understand their moral lives within it. Two important characteristics of the church remain to be explored: the *spirituality* of the church and the *ministerial authority* of the church. These two characteristics are interrelated and easily subject to misperception, but they are key components of a biblical two-kingdoms doctrine.

The first thing to say about the spirituality of the church is probably an emphatic statement about what it is not. The spirituality of the church does *not* mean that the church is antiphysical, antimaterial, or anything along those lines. The church is a visible community that engages in public worship, proclaims the gospel in known languages, baptizes with water, eats bread and drinks wine in remembrance of Christ, follows disciplinary procedures, takes offerings, shows hospitality, and gives material assistance to its poor—and looks forward to the resurrection of the body and the new heaven and new earth. What the spirituality of the church does mean is that the church is a community specially created by Christ and his Holy Spirit, a community that is not defined by or identified with any existing institution or community of the common kingdom. As such the church does not usurp any of the "civil" functions of the common kingdom but devotes itself to exercising its distinctive "spiritual" functions as directed by the Lord Jesus in Scripture. Without a biblical two-kingdoms doctrine it is very difficult to understand and appreciate this important idea. With a biblical two-kingdoms doctrine it should make a great deal of sense.

The spirituality of the church rests upon the fact that the church is a community specially and supernaturally created by Christ and his Holy Spirit. The ideas discussed in previous chapters should be helpful for appreciating this claim. In the Noahic covenant God formally established the common kingdom, and through this kingdom he governs the broad spectrum of human cultural activities and institutions. The church's origins, in contrast, are *not* in the Noahic covenant and *not* in the common kingdom. The Noahic covenant says little specifically about concrete cultural institutions, but it is perfectly reasonable that human beings around the world, living under this covenant, have formed institutions such as courts, schools, and businesses in order to pursue their cultural activities. But the Noahic covenant says nothing about redemption and nothing about a Messiah, and thus the church could never have emerged organically from this covenant. The existence of the church required a new and special initiative of God. Families, governments, schools, and businesses are *natural* institutions, since their origins are in creation or in the Noahic covenant, a covenant that God made with all of nature. But the church is anything but natural. By a *supernatural* divine act Christ announced the establishment of the church: "Blessed are you, Simon Bar-Jonah! For flesh and blood has not revealed this to you, but my Father who is in heaven. And I tell you, you are Peter, and on this rock I will build my church, and the gates of hell shall not prevail against it" (Matt. 16:17–18). Already in the days of Abraham God revealed a new and supernatural initiative of saving grace that promised not the preservation of the common kingdom but a redemptive kingdom bestowing salvation and the life of the world-to-come. This covenant of grace with Abraham came to blessed fulfillment in the coming of Christ and has found its home in the church. Thus the church did not grow out of the soil of the common kingdom but sprang to life out of heaven itself, as the manifestation of a kingdom "not of this world" (John 18:36).

For such reasons it is entirely inappropriate to identify the church with any institution or community of the common kingdom. The church does not owe its existence to any of them and its fate is not linked to any of their fates. All of those institutions and communities, by God's appointment, have an earthly origin and will perish on the day of Christ's return. In contrast, the church has a heavenly origin and will be brought to glorious consummation on the day of Christ like a bride adorned for her husband (Eph. 5:25–33; Rev. 19:9; 21:2).

Following biblical instruction, the church respects and acknowledges these common institutions and communities, but it must never allow itself to be identified with any of them. Things such as families, ethnic background, political allegiance, and socio-economic status define people's identity in the common kingdom and distinguish individuals and groups from one another. The New Testament never says that these distinctions should be banished in the ongoing life of the common kingdom, but it does insist that in the church of Jesus Christ a person's familial, ethnic, political, and economic identities are of no account.[5] Single or married, it does not matter (1 Cor. 7:25–28). Greek, Jew, barbarian, Scythian, it does not matter (Col. 3:11). Slave or free, rich or poor, it does not matter (1 Cor. 7:20–24). Why? Because "Christ is all, and in all" (Col. 3:11), and a person's union with Christ through faith and baptism (Gal. 3:25–29) is the one and only identity that counts in the church. Christianity was never meant to eliminate distinctions in familial, ethnic, political, or economic association. What Christianity was meant to do was to unite people from different families, different ethnic groups, different political factions, and different socio-economic standings into a single community, "baptized into one body—Jews or Greeks, slaves or free . . ." (1 Cor. 12:13).

Through the two thousand years of church history the identification of the church (or parts thereof) with nation-states, ethnic groups, and political factions has proven to be an especially serious temptation and snare. The historical examples are far too numerous

---

[5]One exception to this statement, with respect to the family, is that young children of believers are reckoned as holy in God's sight, and thus as members of the church, as discussed briefly in chapter 5.

to mention. In our own day, in the American context in which I write, various churches' identification with particular political causes or political parties, with particular economic agendas, with American military success, or simply with (idealized) American culture has been widely discussed and debated. It must be said emphatically that the church long predated America, will long survive America, and at present should view America, the world's lone superpower, as another "drop from a bucket" (Isa. 40:15). I do not claim that the church has nothing relevant to say about politics, economics, war, or other such things. Later in this chapter and in chapter 7 I will discuss what the church can and should say about them. For the moment I offer two preliminary suggestions for helping the church guard her true spiritual character and avoid entanglement and identification with the fleeting institutions and communities of this world.

First, the church may wish to test itself by asking whether something it does or teaches necessarily excludes some Christians from participating in its life and worship because of their ethnic or national identity (political identity is more complicated, and I will save that discussion for later). At first thought this might not seem to be a very helpful test of a church's fidelity to its spiritual character, since the limits of time and space necessarily exclude most Christians from most worship services most of the time. Churches must meet at a particular time and location and speak a particular language, and the vast majority of Christians, who reside somewhere else and/ or speak a different language will not be able to participate. But let us imagine that one Christian is randomly chosen from all of the Christians in the world and dropped into an American worship service (and given the ability to understand the language). Here is the test that I suggest: does the minister say anything in his sermon to which this Christian cannot say "amen," is there any phrase in any of the songs which this Christian cannot sing, or is there any visual prop that causes discomfort or offence to this Christian, on account of this Christian's ethnic or national affiliation?

If the minister prays for the peace and prosperity of America, this Christian from a foreign land should have no difficulty saying "amen," since Scripture straightforwardly instructs believers to pray in this manner (e.g., see Jer. 29:7; 1 Tim. 2:1–2) and surely no Christian should wish war and poverty upon fellow believers anywhere in the world. Likewise, if the minister prays for a just resolution to an international dispute in which America is involved, this Christian should also be able to respond with "amen," for what Christian would not wish justice to be done everywhere in the world?

But now we might imagine that the minister prays for America's victory in an international dispute or that the congregation is asked to sing a patriotic American song after the sermon (perhaps this Christian just happens to visit America on Fourth of July weekend). What if her own native country is the one having the dispute with America, and her own livelihood and security are at stake? What if she feels patriotic sentiments for her own country and has no interest in expressing patriotism for America? She would be unable to yield her "amen" to such proceedings, and this would be perfectly understandable—just as understandable as an American worshiping in a Russian church and feeling disinclined to pray for the triumph of Russian foreign policy or to sing patriotic Russian songs. When we are immersed in our own culture and own national interests, it is often difficult to realize how often we attach the church's identity to a national or ethnic identity, and hence to betray the spirituality of the church. The scenarios that I have imagined might cause us to pause and to reflect upon how the church can do better at living as though there really is no Jew, Greek, barbarian, or Scythian within its walls.

My second preliminary suggestion for guarding the spirituality of the church is to ask whether a church's activities are usurping the legitimate authority given by God to another institution or community in the common kingdom. As noted, when Jesus came, he did not establish a family, a state, a school, or a business, but the church alone. These other institutions already existed under divine authority through the Noahic covenant as aspects of the common kingdom. It is theoretically possible, of course, that Jesus might have created his church to take over the responsibilities that these institutions had previously exercised, making the church an all-encompassing social organization. But he did not do this. As considered in chapter 5, Jesus and the New Testament writers affirmed the importance of institutions like the family and the state and acknowledged *their* continuing authority over matters long ago entrusted to them. The tasks that the New Testament does ascribe to the church are, not surprisingly, tasks that institutions of the common kingdom were not already performing and were not competent to perform: exercising the keys of the kingdom (Matt. 16:18–19), conducting discipline according to the Sermon on the Mount (Matt. 18:15–17), baptizing and making disciples of Christ (Matt. 28:19–20), preaching the gospel (2 Tim. 4:1–5), celebrating the Lord's Supper (1 Cor. 11:17–34), and ordaining ministers (1 Tim. 4:14; Titus 1:5–9). (One task entrusted to the church, diaconal aid to the poor [Acts 6:1–6; 1 Tim. 5:3–16], does overlap with the work of some institutions of the common kingdom, and I will discuss this in the next section.)

Thus a good practice for the church to follow, I suggest, is to keep asking itself about each thing that it does: is this *its own proper* work, or did God entrust this work to another, nonecclesiastical institution? The church would surely not be pleased if the state began to administer baptism or if a business ordained a minister to preach the gospel. The church should be equally suspicious about its own claims to arbitrate civil justice (like the state) or to sell commercial products in the marketplace (like a business). If the church is to retain its spiritual character it must be zealous for doing its own special work well (which the church has found to be difficult enough) and to leave other work for the institutions to which God has entrusted it.

These preliminary suggestions for guarding the spirituality of the church have surely not answered all particular questions about the church's teaching and activities in relation to the institutions and communities of the common kingdom. In order to address some of these more particular questions I believe it is helpful to consider the ministerial authority of the church.

The Ministerial Authority of the Church
The idea that the church has only *ministerial* authority can be defined rather simply: the officers of the church[6] have authority

---

[6]By the "officers of the church," I refer to the New Testament offices of minister (primarily entrusted with tasks of preaching and teaching), elder (entrusted with tasks of governing the church's affairs

only to minister what the Word of God teaches, not to make up their own doctrines for believing or rules for living, no matter how compelling or wise they might seem to be. Ministerial authority stands in contrast to *legislative* authority, which leaders in the common kingdom possess. While the state, for example, has a broad discretionary power to *make* laws, the church has only the power to *declare* the laws and doctrines that already appear in Scripture. In short, church officers can say and do only that which Scripture authorizes them to say and do. At first this may sound constricting and burdensome for the church, but its effect and driving motivation is actually to protect the *liberty* of Christians. If church officers cannot teach anything beyond what Scripture teaches, then they are unable to bind the consciences of Christians beyond how Scripture already binds it. Thus Christian liberty is maximized. Christian consciences are bound to believe and to do as Scripture instructs, but Christians are free to exercise their own wisdom in deciding how to live and what to think about all matters that Scripture does not address (within the bounds of respecting other legitimate authority structures in society).[7] I might also add that this idea should be liberating for pastors. They do not need to be experts on everything from the pulpit. They have only one simple but profound responsibility: ministering the Word of God.

Some historical context might be helpful. At the time of the Reformation, Protestants believed that the Roman church was widely guilty of usurping authority that it did not rightly possess by imposing practices and doctrines not taught in Scripture. The Roman church, for example, taught that Christians should not eat meat on Fridays, thus seeking to bind Christian consciences on a matter about

---

and of overseeing the spiritual well-being of the flock), and deacon (entrusted with ministries of benevolence and mercy). Though all members of the church may perform some of these tasks in an informal way, the church's officers perform them in an "official" way and thus speak or act with the authority of Christ himself. This is why the question of *how* they exercise their authority is so important. This understanding of church offices reflects my own Presbyterian convictions. For a detailed discussion of such issues, see, e.g., Herman Bavinck, *Reformed Dogmatics*, vol. 4, *Holy Spirit, Church, and New Creation*, ed. John Bolt, trans. John Vriend (Grand Rapids: Baker, 2008), chap. 6.

[7]For an important Reformation-era discussion of this general topic, see John Calvin, *Institutes of the Christian Religion*, 4.10–11.

which Scripture was silent. Over against such things, Protestants would respond that eating meat on Fridays is a matter *indifferent* in and of itself. Neither eating meat nor not eating meat is inherently good or evil, and thus the church cannot lay down rules one way or the other. This does not mean that a decision about eating meat on Friday has no moral value. All sorts of moral factors may be relevant for such a decision (such as a person's health or financial resources), but the point is that individuals (or parents, or physicians), *not the officers of the church*, should be making these moral decisions. This doctrine, if appreciated and practiced, has tremendous implications for the character of the church as well as for the Christian's conduct in the broader cultural world.

Before reflecting specifically on these implications, I offer a brief biblical defense of the ministerial authority of the church. As with the doctrine of the spirituality of the church, the idea of the church's ministerial authority is much easier to understand if viewed in light of the two-kingdoms doctrine. To begin, recall that the institutions of the common kingdom, unlike the church, arose out of the covenant with Noah (or in some cases at creation). The authority structures in these institutions emerge from natural relationships and have a very general character. In Genesis 1 and again in Genesis 9, for example, God instructs the human race to "be fruitful and multiply," but he never specifically gives parents authority over their children. In Genesis 9, God prescribes that "whoever sheds the blood of man, by man shall his blood be shed," but he never specifically gives civil magistrates authority over the people. At later points in history Scripture acknowledges that parents and civil magistrates have such authority and encourages obedience to them (e.g., Ex. 20:12; Rom. 13:1–7), but parenthood and civil government had already been in existence and exercised legitimate authority for a long time by then. The written Scriptures *confirm* their authority but did not *create* it. Parents and civil magistrates did not need to wait for Scripture to be written in order to exercise their authority. Authority in the common kingdom emerged out of natural relationships (such as parent-child, magistrate-people, employer-employee, and teacher-student), which were based in covenants with nature that God made at creation and later through Noah. Therefore the authority possessed by parents, magistrates, and others is very general (not able to be precisely defined). Parents and magistrates should make rules and laws that seem appropriate given the nature of their relationships and the needs of particular circumstances.

Because the church is *not* a natural institution grounded in creation or the Noahic covenant, however, its authority structures could not emerge organically from natural relationships. Neither could the nature of its officers' authority be logically derived from natural necessities. The church was specially and supernaturally established by Christ (Matt. 16:17–19). Only Christ, therefore, by his own words and the words of his inspired apostles, could establish the authority structures in the church and the scope of church officers' authority. Christ has in fact done exactly this by appointing the offices of pastor, elder, and deacon and defining the qualifications and responsibilities for holding these offices (e.g., Acts 6:1–6; 14:23; 20:17–35; Eph. 4:11–12; 1 Tim. 3:1–13; 4:6–16; 5:17–22; 2 Tim. 2:1–7, 14–16, 22–26; 4:1–5; Titus 1:5–9; 2:1–15). The offices come from Christ as made known in the New Testament and thus their authority comes from Christ as made known in the New Testament.

When church officers seek to do things or to impose doctrines or practices that Scripture does not authorize, they usurp authority rather than exercise the authority that Christ has given. Jesus warned against religious leaders who teach "as doctrines the commandments of men" (Matt. 15:9), and Paul warned against those who impart "human precepts and teachings" which have "an appearance of wisdom in promoting self-made religion . . ." (Col. 2:22–23). At times, of course, the church must establish certain rules that are not explicitly in Scripture, to make it possible to carry out commands that are in Scripture (e.g., setting a time and place for everyone to meet in order to keep biblical commands about worshiping together in good order; see 1 Cor. 14:40). But church officers must be zealous for doing and teaching all that Scripture authorizes and, as far as possible, leaving Christians with the liberty to do and to believe what they deem best in all matters that Scripture leaves open. No

Christian should "pass judgment" or "quarrel over opinions" with another Christian (Rom. 14:1–3).

The concrete implications of this principle for the life and ministry of the church are vast. Scripture instructs Christians to be submissive to civil authorities but does not provide strategies for voting or reforming public policy. Scripture instructs Christians to discipline their children but does not tell them what methods to use. Scripture instructs Christians to train their children but does not tell them what schools they should attend or what the best pedagogical methods are. Scripture tells Christians to work diligently and honestly at their earthly occupations but does not tell them how to run their businesses or how to handle stress on the job. If a church and its leaders take seriously their *ministerial authority*, then they will exhort Christians to do what Scripture instructs and leave them at liberty to make wise and responsible decisions about the other things.[8] Church officers should teach Christians to submit to civil authorities, to discipline and educate their children, and to work diligently and honestly. They should offer them pastoral counsel to help them grow in wisdom in such areas. But they should not command them what political strategies to follow, what child-rearing methods to utilize, or how to make their businesses run more efficiently. In chapter 7 we will consider in more detail how Christians should approach and make godly decisions about education, vocation, and politics in light of this.

I close this section by briefly considering two specific issues that are often the source of controversy in churches: what to do in worship and how to administer the church's diaconal or benevolence ministry. The two-kingdoms doctrine and the idea of the ministerial authority of the church do not give an immediate answer for every particular question about these issues, but they do provide some very important guidance for churches seeking to handle them in a God-pleasing way.

---

[8]To avoid possible misunderstanding, I would add that church officers, out of pastoral concern, should help their flock to grow in wisdom and to think through important (though extrabiblical) moral decisions, without imposing their own judgments upon members' consciences.

First, the fact that the church's authority is ministerial indicates that the church should worship in ways that the New Testament instructs the church to worship and not in other ways. This idea is sometimes referred to as the *regulative principle of worship*— Scripture alone regulates the worship of the church.[9] We should be clear what this means. Presumably all Christians would agree in theory that the church should worship in ways that the New Testament commands and should not worship in ways that the New Testament prohibits. But may the church worship in ways that the New Testament neither prohibits nor commands?[10] Many Christians answer yes, believing that worship services may include things like dramatic skits, liturgical dances, or service-project reports if the pastor or a worship team thinks that they will be interesting and edifying, even though the New Testament never instructs churches to worship in these ways.

If the church's authority is ministerial, however, this conclusion is problematic. The church should strive to worship only in ways that the New Testament prescribes. The reason is rather simple. Since Scripture teaches that Christians must gather for corporate worship (Heb. 10:24–25), churches, through their ministers and elders, must call their members together for worship services, and these members must participate. It is not optional for churches to have worship services and it is not optional for Christians to attend. Likewise, nothing that happens during the worship service should be optional or designed to exclude some people—everyone should be edified and able to say "amen" to everything that transpires (1 Cor. 14:16–17). But since the church's authority is only ministerial, it cannot make

---

[9]For a concise explanation of some terminology that helps to explain what the regulative principle of worship means, see also T. David Gordon, "The Westminster Assembly's Unworkable and Un-scriptural View of Worship?" *Westminster Theological Journal* 65 (2003): 347–50.

[10]My reference to the "church" and the "New Testament" here are significant. What Scripture says about *private* worship and *Old Testament* worship cannot be automatically applied to the New Testament church's corporate worship. There is much to learn about worship from the Old Testament, but many aspects of Old Testament worship are no longer appropriate after Christ's coming (as Hebrews explains), so we must look to the New Testament to know what is fitting now. Also, not all that is appropriate elsewhere in life can be assumed to be appropriate in the church's corporate worship (e.g., 1 Cor. 14:33–35). Dancing, an example I mention in the text, is a means of worship in the Old Testament, and may still be appropriate privately, but is never commanded as part of New Testament corporate worship.

Christians say "amen" to things that are not taught in Scripture. Whether a liturgical dance or a dramatic skit is edifying is a matter of personal judgment. Some people may say "amen" and others may say "no thanks." For a pastor or a worship team to impose such practices on corporate worship is therefore to force all Christians to agree with their own personal opinions. This is usurping authority and violates Christians' liberty. In contrast, things that Scripture says should be done in corporate worship—such as the reading and preaching of the Word, praying and singing, and celebrating the Lord's Supper (e.g., Acts 2:42; 1 Cor. 11:17–34; 14:26; 1 Tim. 4:13)[11]—are not matters of personal judgment. Because they are biblical, all Christians should be able to say "amen" to these things.

Some people mistakenly think that this regulative principle of worship is a burdensome restriction on the church. As a matter of fact, adhering to this principle promotes a proper sense of Christian liberty. It protects each and every Christian from having other people's personal opinions imposed upon them when they gather for worship at the Lord's command. Christians are free on their own to seek to honor God through dances and drama, but they should not force others to engage in them.

Second and finally, the fact that the church's authority is ministerial indicates that its diaconal or benevolence work should be conducted in ways that Scripture directs, and not otherwise. Scripture often encourages believers to help the needy, but what this means for the church's diaconal work can be controversial. Should the church start a soup kitchen or medical clinic in a poor neighborhood? Should it pursue community economic development as well as preaching the gospel in third-world mission fields? The doctrine of the church's ministerial authority provides a guiding principle when the church faces such questions: the church, acting officially through its deacons, has authority to do only the kind of diaconal work that Christ, speaking in Scripture, authorizes it to do.

---

[11] Though extraordinary gifts—such as speaking in tongues—were evidently practiced in worship services in at least some congregations of the very early church, Scripture gives good reason to believe that we should not be practicing these gifts in the church today. For a defense of this position see, e.g., Richard B. Gaffin, *Perspectives on Pentecost: New Testament Teaching on the Gifts of the Holy Spirit* (Phillipsburg, NJ: Presbyterian and Reformed, 1979).

When the New Testament gives instructions about diaconal work, it authorizes the church to give material assistance to the needy *of the church* and not the needy of the world in general. This is first evident in Acts 6:1–6. The seven men appointed in this story are not called "deacons," but the work they are given—"to serve tables" in support of widows—is diaconal in nature and foreshadows the work that deacons would do. According to the instruction of the apostles, these men are chosen by the church in order to ensure that needy widows among "the disciples" are provided for. Later in the New Testament Paul speaks about the church's mercy ministry for the needy on several occasions, and they all concern benevolence for the *Christian* poor. In 1 Corinthians 16:1–4 and 2 Corinthians 8–9, for example, Paul encourages the church in Corinth to take offerings that would be sent to "the saints" (see 1 Cor. 16:1; 2 Cor. 9:1) in Jerusalem who were suffering material want. (These passages are an important reminder that the church's diaconal ministry to needy Christians should have an international as well as a local perspective.) In 1 Timothy 5:3–16, furthermore, where Paul gives detailed instructions to the church about providing material assistance to widows, his instructions make clear that only Christian widows should be on the roll of those receiving aid. These widows must have "washed the feet of the saints" and been "devoted . . . to every good work," and the church must take care lest widows they assist be drawn "away from Christ." The New Testament, however, never commands the church's diaconal work to assist people outside the church. What the New Testament authorizes, therefore, is that the church's diaconal ministry should be directed toward needy Christians.

This conclusion should not be misunderstood. Scripture commands Christians to love and care for their neighbors, whether they are believers or not. Paul says, for example, "As we have opportunity, let us do good to everyone, and especially to those who are of the household of faith" (Gal. 6:10). While the passages mentioned in the previous paragraph instruct the official diaconal work of the church to be focused upon the Christian poor, Galatians 6:10 and many other verses command all Christians in their own lives to be loving and generous toward all people. Institutions of the common kingdom such as families, businesses, and states often provide care for the poor of this world, and Christians should consider how they can participate in this work. Individual Christians and groups of Christians may choose to set up their own community soup kitchens, medical clinics, and job-training centers. Physicians and nurses may choose to show Christian love for their neighbors through offering medical care for the poor, lawyers may choose to show it through doing *pro bono* legal work, and carpenters and electricians may choose to show it through constructing homes for the homeless. Many Christians are already involved in wonderful organizations, independent of the church, that do such work. Such organizations—administered by people with expertise in medicine, law, or construction—are better equipped than the church to do these tasks, for the elders and deacons who are supposed to administer the church's work do not necessarily have expertise in any of these fields (1 Tim. 3:1–13).

The church's nature is spiritual and its authority is ministerial, thus it should not take up cultural tasks that Scripture has not entrusted to it. Just because Christians should be doing certain things does not mean that the church itself should do them. The church's diaconal work should focus upon care for its own poor—it has a hard enough time doing this well (especially from an international perspective). Believers, however, according to the abilities, resources, and opportunities they have, should extend the love of Christ to all their neighbors, and the church should not bind their consciences about when and how they do so.

Conclusion

This chapter has covered a lot of ground in considering the church as the redemptive kingdom and the way of the Christian life within it. I have argued that the church's worship and fellowship should be central to the Christian life and that the character of the church's worship and fellowship should be strikingly distinctive from the ethic of earthly institutions. I have explained the spirituality of the church and the ministerial authority of the church, furthermore, as helpful guides for showing the church what sorts of things the church should say and do and what sorts of things it should not.

Thus we have explored the Christian life in the redemptive kingdom. But what about the Christian life in the common kingdom? Christians should hold the church closest to their hearts—closer than family, country, or business—but they still have important tasks in the common kingdom and are called to honor God by pursuing them well. The church, we have seen, should encourage all Christians to take up these tasks faithfully while leaving it to their own wisdom as to how to carry them out. In the final chapter we will consider in more depth what the Christian life might look like in three important areas of the common kingdom: education, vocation, and politics.

Education, Vocation, and Politics

IN THIS CONCLUDING CHAPTER we arrive at last at the specific issues that probably prompted many readers to pick up this book in the first place. How exactly should Christians perform their various cultural activities in the broader world, and does the two-kingdoms doctrine have anything useful to say about this? How should Christians view important endeavors such as learning, work, and political involvement? There is no shortage of books that address the relationship of Christianity with education, vocation, and politics. But it is difficult to find a sustained treatment of such subjects from the perspective of a two-kingdoms doctrine as I have defended and explored it in the previous chapters. Though a biblical two-kingdoms doctrine does not, by itself, tell us everything there is to know about these subjects, it has immensely important things to contribute to discussions about Christian cultural engagement. For one thing, it can help us to avoid two extreme and incorrect perspectives: on the one hand, that activities such as education, work, and politics can be simplistically slotted as "Christian" or "non-Christian" (which fails to recognize the *common dimension* of these activities) and, on the other hand, that our Christian faith has nothing to do with such activities (which fails to recognize the *fundamental religious antithesis* that affects every area of life).

For many readers, I suspect, my conclusions and suggestions in this chapter will resonate with the way you already think about and perform your cultural activities in the broader world, and the two-kingdoms doctrine will provide you with helpful biblical categories for better understanding and articulating what you already suspected was true. For other readers, undoubtedly, this chapter will present a fundamental challenge to the way in which you view (or have been told to view) your studying, working, and voting.

Whatever the case may be, I hope that this chapter will provide a stimulating and charitable contribution to ongoing debates about the nature of Christian involvement in cultural enterprises. I will pick up on important themes that have been running through this book, namely, that Christians have a responsibility to be involved in a broad range of cultural endeavors, that they can and should honor God by their righteous pursuit of such activities, and that they should perform these activities, as activities of the common kingdom under the Noahic covenant, alongside of and in cooperation with unbelievers. *Christians are Christians seven days a week*, in whatever place or activity they find themselves, and thus they must always strive to live consistently with their profession of Christ. At the same time, we should be careful about how we use the term "Christian" to describe our education, work, politics, or other cultural endeavors. While Scripture has significant things to say about all of our cultural endeavors, it does not tell us everything about any of them. Scripture provides a general, big-picture perspective about these endeavors but does not ordinarily provide specific instructions about how to pursue them in an excellent and socially beneficial way. God therefore leaves much to the wisdom and discretion of Christians as they make their way in the common kingdom and interact with unbelieving colleagues. Every Christian has the obligation to make morally responsible decisions about his cultural endeavors. But Christians must also be on guard against condemning other Christians' decisions about matters for which Scripture does not bind the conscience. We should be modest about claiming our own decisions and views about such things as the Christian view.

I hope that readers will find the conclusions of this chapter (and the book as a whole) to be both *liberating* and *weighty*. The conclusions are liberating, I believe, because they claim that Christians' consciences cannot be bound by the extrabiblical demands of fellow believers who seek to impose the "Christian" way of teaching mathematics to our children, running our businesses, or supporting political candidates. The conclusions are also weighty, however, because this Christian liberty, which unshackles our consciences from other people's nonbiblical demands, puts the responsibility back upon ourselves. Our pastors and elders have not been called to micromanage our cultural activities, though sometimes we might wish that we could shift to somebody else the responsibility of deciding how to educate our children, whether to fire a difficult employee, or whether to support a candidate's political campaign. In the end these are decisions that we must make as individuals and as families with the wisdom God gives us as we live out our Christian faith in our own particular life circumstances. (Though this responsibility is weighty, however, it should not be overwhelming. We may seek counsel and encouragement from fellow believers when we struggle with difficult decisions. Most importantly, we make these decisions as people already justified in Christ, the last Adam, who has offered perfect obedience to the Father on our behalf, and thus loves us and accepts us even when we fail to make the wisest decisions.)

In order to explain and defend such conclusions, I will unfold this chapter in four sections. First I address some general issues regarding the Christian's cultural work, as I build upon my claims in previous chapters. Then I discuss in turn three major areas of Christian cultural activity: education, vocation, and politics. In each case I will consider what Scripture says about these activities and also how Christians might begin to think through their moral decisions in areas where Scripture is silent.

Christians' Cultural Activity: Joyful, Detached, Modest

Before we examine several specific cultural activities, it is important to reflect briefly upon some general issues at stake in the present discussion. The first section of this chapter, therefore, draws upon the biblical-theological material developed over the previous five chapters and describes the basic attitude and perspective with which Christians should approach their life in the common kingdom. As suggested toward the end of chapter 5, I believe that *joy, detachment,* and *modesty* (about what we think we can accomplish and what we claim to be doing) are fitting words to describe this perspective.

When seeking to develop a proper perspective on cultural activity in the common kingdom, Christians do well first to remember that they are not new Adams. Redemption in Christ does not place Christians back in the garden of Eden and does not impose Adam's original cultural obligation upon them. As explored in chapters 2 and 3, God originally commissioned Adam to image him by being fruitful and multiplying and by exercising dominion over the world, with the goal of attaining a new creation, a new heaven and new earth, if he obeyed this commission. When Adam failed and plunged the world into sin and condemnation, God's work of salvation did not restore us to Adam's original position and give us a second chance to fulfill Adam's task. Instead, God sent his only Son, our Lord Jesus Christ, as the second and last Adam, who passed a test like the one Adam failed and has thus entered the new creation. Those who trust in Christ have already become citizens of heaven and are assured that they will one day enter the new heaven and new earth solely on account of the last Adam's work. Christians therefore *are in no way bringing in the new creation by their cultural activities.* To take such a view is to compromise the finality and sufficiency of Christ's perfect obedience on earth and his glorious entry into the glory of heaven. The new creation has been earned and attained by the work of Christ the last Adam alone.

As we have also seen, especially in chapters 4–5, though we are not little Adams we still have many cultural responsibilities here and now. God does not call Christians to take up the original cultural mandate of Genesis 1:26–28 per se, but calls them to obey the cultural mandate *as given in modified form to Noah* in Genesis 9. Through the Noahic covenant God formally established the common kingdom and commissioned all people—believers and unbelievers alike—to be fruitful and multiply and to exercise dominion on earth.

The goal of this commission is not to provide a way to earn or to attain the new creation but to foster the temporary preservation of life and social order until the end of the present world. According to the terms of this covenant, Christians—and indeed all people—are morally accountable to God in their cultural work. Christians should bring honor to God as they pursue a range of cultural endeavors in the common kingdom. As they do so, the terms of this covenant also remind them that they should support legitimate social institutions (such as the family and the state) and must labor in coordination and cooperation with unbelievers (even while they maintain fundamental religious disagreements with them).

Christians, furthermore, should pursue cultural activities of the common kingdom with a genuine sense of joy and satisfaction. Drudgery and disappointment frequently afflict such activities. Students often find school frustrating, workers often find their jobs tedious, and voters often find the political process discouraging. Nevertheless, Ecclesiastes encourages us to eat and drink with joy, to find enjoyment in our labor, and to revel in family life, insofar as God bestows these things upon us in the midst of life's many frustrations (e.g., Eccles. 2:24; 9:7–9). Such cultural activities are good, honorable, and God-ordained. As divine gifts they should be pursued with excellence.

When I reflected on this point in chapter 5, however, I also noted that the New Testament says little to reaffirm this perspective. Though the description of life "under the sun" in Ecclesiastes remains essentially applicable for us today, finding joy and satisfaction in cultural activities is simply not a major theme of the New Testament. It is not really a theme of the New Testament at all. Again and again the New Testament reminds us that while cultural life goes on by God's appointment, it is temporary and of relative importance in comparison to the perfect work of Christ, the flourishing of the church, and the hope of the world-to-come. According to the New Testament, Christians should work hard and submit to legitimate authorities in the common kingdom. Yet they should pursue their cultural activities with a sense of detachment that qualifies their joy and satisfaction in them. Their joy and satisfaction in cultural accomplishments should be nothing compared to the wonder of being a citizen of heaven and an heir of eternal life. Our families, schools, businesses, and civil governments are good and legitimate, but also temporary and transitory. Our joy in cultural activities is a pilgrim joy, a joy of exiles and sojourners. It is not an ultimate joy but a joy of quiet gratitude for small blessings that God bestows for a time.

At this point I pause for a moment to reflect on a common misconception about the proper Christian attitude toward cultural endeavors. Many recent books on Christianity and culture target sayings such as "you don't polish the brass on a sinking ship," which some people use to denigrate cultural work based upon the idea that it's all about to be destroyed anyway. Such sayings are indeed unhelpful and misleading, and recent books are correct to look for a different perspective. But often the alternative that writers present is that the ship is not sinking at all. The ship is our everlasting home and is being transformed through redemption in Christ, and thus our cultural efforts to improve the ship are fashioning the new creation itself. As considered in chapter 3, however, "the present form of this world is passing away" (1 Cor. 7:31). Our cultural activities—like marriage and commerce (1 Cor. 7:29–30)—are honorable. They have eternal consequences in that God will recognize our good deeds on the last day and give to us our due (e.g., 2 Cor. 5:9–10). But our cultural products themselves are not meant to endure into the world-to-come. They belong to the stuff of the present world. Contrary to what some people suggest, we *are* to spend time on things that do not last. We are like the Israelite exiles, who built homes and planted gardens in Babylon, though they knew they would leave there after seventy years.

The final issue for this section is whether or in what way our cultural activities are "Christian." This is a difficult and potentially contentious matter, in part because of confusion about terminology. I believe that this issue basically asks us to specify what is and what is not *unique* about *Christians'* work in the common kingdom. A two-kingdoms doctrine distinguishes what is uniquely "Christian" from what is simply "human." Sometimes people assert that to be a Christian is to be truly human, and in one sense this is true. Through the work of Christ Christians attain the original destiny of the human race: life in the world-to-come. But precisely for this reason we should not equate what is "Christian" with what is generically "human" in the present world. Generally speaking, to be "human" here and now means living in the common kingdom under the Noahic covenant. Christians share the life and activities of the common kingdom with all human beings. What differentiates them from the rest of humanity is their identification with the redemptive kingdom and all that that entails. Thus in this chapter I use the adjective "Christian" not to describe everything that should characterize human beings in this world, but to describe what differentiates Christians from the rest of humanity and thus makes them unique.

I suggest that there are many unique things about Christians' cultural activities but that a variety of factors encourage us to be modest in claiming the "Christian" title for those things that we do and accomplish in the common kingdom. First of all, believers must strive to perform all of their cultural activities in a way consistent with their Christian identity, and this means, as a *subjective* matter, that the Christian's cultural activities should always be fundamentally different from unbelievers'. Christians are called not only to act in accord with God's law at all times but also to do all things from faith (Rom. 14:23; Heb. 11:6) and all things for God's glory (1 Cor. 10:31). Though unbelievers do many things that are in outward conformity to God's law (when they are honest, refrain from violence and adultery, etc.), they never truly exhibit faith in Christ as a foundation for their actions or seek God's glory as the goal of their conduct. Here then is one way in which cultural activity should be uniquely *Christian*: even in their most ordinary and mundane tasks, Christians must act from faith, in accord with God's law, and for God's glory. Whatever they do, they should "work heartily, as for the Lord and not for men" (Col. 3:23). An unbeliever can never and will never do this. Because of Christians' inner motivation and subjective attitude, therefore, they should always be interpreting their cultural activities differently from unbelievers, hence making their cultural work, in this respect, uniquely Christian.

Looking at this issue as an *objective* matter is more difficult and requires a nuanced answer. Generally speaking, believers are not to seek an objectively unique Christian way of pursuing cultural activities. This is true for several interrelated reasons.

First, the normative standards for cultural activities are, in general, not *distinctively* Christian. By this I mean that the moral requirements that we expect of Christians in cultural work are ordinarily the same moral requirements that we expect of non-Christians, and the standards of excellence for such work are the same for believers and unbelievers. If you have ever asked someone who promotes "Christian" cultural activity what that Christian activity should look like, that person has probably said something like the following: Christians should be honest, just, hardworking, environmentally responsible, and respectful to authority.[1] Christians should certainly act in these ways, as many statements in the Bible indicate. But perhaps you have also stopped to consider whether these characteristics are uniquely Christian. If we hire a non-Christian plumber to work in our home or hire a non-Christian employee at our shop, for example, would we expect the same sort of behavior from them? Undoubtedly we would! These characteristics are not unique Christian obligations but are universal human obligations. Chapter 4 explained that God entered into covenant with all human beings in his covenant with Noah in Genesis 9, when he formally established the common kingdom. All human beings continue to bear the image of God (albeit in corrupted form) and are morally obligated to him. They continue to know the basic moral law of God through natural revelation even if they have never read Scripture (see Rom. 1:18–32; 2:14–15). Through the Noahic covenant God holds all people accountable for being honest, just, hardworking, environmentally responsible, and respectful to authority.

To understand this point better we might reflect upon a few moral obligations that *are* uniquely Christian. Participating in the Lord's

---

[1] See below for examples of writers who say these sorts of things.

Supper and "turning the other cheek," for example, are obligations known *only* through Scripture and are binding *only* upon citizens of Christ's heavenly kingdom. The Lord's Supper is a confirmation of one's faith in Christ, and those who do not have such faith should absolutely *not* partake (1 Cor. 11:27). Turning the other cheek rather than enforcing an "eye for an eye" is specifically commanded of Jesus' followers insofar as they are citizens of the kingdom of heaven (Matt. 5:38–42[2]) (while the requirement of enforcing an "eye for an eye" as a principle of justice is binding upon the human race generally in the common kingdom, according to Gen. 9:6). Participating in the Lord's Supper and turning the other cheek when persecuted for the faith are truly "Christian" moral obligations. Being honest, hardworking, and just, on the other hand, are simply human moral obligations. Christians have a different motive for pursuing them, for they alone pursue humility and industriousness as an expression of their faith in Christ and for the goal of honoring God. We would also hope that Christians perform these moral obligations better than non-Christians, though sadly we know that this is often not true. Frequently our non-Christian colleagues are more honest and hardworking than our Christian colleagues.

Second, along similar lines, the standards of excellence for cultural work are generally the same for believers and unbelievers. What constitutes excellence for the Christian engineer? Whether the bridge he designs holds up traffic. What constitutes excellence for the Christian plumber? Whether the pipes he fixes stop leaking. Once again we might ask the question: would we hold a non-Christian engineer or plumber to the same standards? Absolutely. Activities such as building bridges and repairing broken pipes are general human activities, not uniquely Christian ones. Because God has upheld the natural order and sustained all human beings as his image-bearers through the Noahic covenant, these are activities of the common kingdom. The technical aspects of our cultural labors—those things that distinguish excellent work from mediocre work from shoddy work—do not depend on what is uniquely

---

[2]See chapter 5 for an extended discussion of the Sermon on the Mount.

Christian. Christ's resurrection, ascension, and establishment of the church have not changed the truths of calculus or the way that water flows. The fact that a plumber is converted to Christianity does not change his objective obligations as a plumber (even though he now has new motivation for being industrious and honest as he pursues his vocation).

It is therefore unhelpful to describe our common kingdom activities in terms of "transformation," and it is inaccurate to describe them in terms of "redemption." Christians must think critically about the claims and activities of unbelievers (and believers) in the common kingdom, for the sinful mind and heart continually seek ways to pervert truth and morality. Scripture is crucial for this critical thinking, serving as the lens through which we most clearly recognize sin and corruption. But even when we uncover and correct serious distortions in human cultural activity, we are still dealing with the activities of *this world* and the affairs of the *common kingdom*. We do not seek a uniquely Christian way to perform these activities and order these affairs, but we conduct ourselves as sojourners and exiles who share them in common with unbelievers and do not really feel at home when pursuing them. We desire to make the common kingdom better when we can, but we should not try to "transform" it into something other than the common kingdom. We rejoice when our cultural activity contributes to making the common kingdom more just and prosperous, but we are not called to "redeem" it, as if God is saving the common kingdom rather than simply preserving it temporarily.

Third, seeking an objectively unique "Christian" way of pursuing cultural activities is potentially hazardous in light of the fact that there are usually *many possible* ways in which Christians could pursue such activities. As discussed, the same basic moral requirements and standards of excellence bind believers and unbelievers, and believers might have legitimate disagreements with one another about how to perform tasks in the common kingdom. Scripture speaks at a broad, general level about all cultural activities, but it says little or nothing about the concrete details of activities such as working and voting. Making concrete decisions about these activities requires wisdom and judgment in light of the varying circumstances in which we find ourselves. As considered in chapter 6, where Scripture does not bind the conscience, Christians should not bind each others' consciences. Consider Christians who own small businesses. Presumably they spend most of their time pondering not whether to be honest or industrious, but how to market their products, whether to hire or fire certain people, how to reduce their tax bill, and whether to open a new location. No two Christians would make exactly the same decisions about such problems, yet we would not conclude that only one of them (at most) has discovered *the* Christian way to run a small business. We might well conclude that many of them have run their businesses in ways consistent with their Christian confession. But for one of them to claim that hers is a "Christian" business, when another Christian could legitimately make very different decisions about running the business, is stretching the usefulness of such language.

What conclusions can be drawn at this point in the chapter? Because the common kingdom will remain the common kingdom until Christ returns, and because the objective normative standards for cultural activities will ordinarily be common to believers and unbelievers until the end of the present world, Christians should strive for modesty and honesty in cultural affairs. Christians should be modest in their expectations about what they can accomplish with regard to the cultural institutions of the present world. We can contribute in many small ways to making the common kingdom a better place, and occasionally we can be instrumental in forging large, systemic improvements to our cultural environment. But the fact that the common kingdom will remain the common kingdom should instill a profound modesty and humility in us. Whatever contributions we make, small or great, are contributions to a cultural arena that is temporary and fleeting.

The language that we use in describing this work should be correspondingly modest and humble. We would do well, I believe, to discard familiar mantras about "transformation" and especially "redemption." Nowhere does Scripture call us to such grandiose tasks. They are human dreams rather than God-given obligations.

Similarly, we do well to be appropriately cautious about our use of the term "Christian" to describe our cultural work. Our presuppositions, big-picture perspective, and motivation concerning cultural activities certainly ought to be "Christian" in the full and unique sense of the term. But since the basic moral requirements that obligate us and the technical standards that constitute excellence in various crafts are ordinarily common to believers and unbelievers, and since believers themselves may legitimately disagree with one another about the concrete details of how to pursue cultural activities, then using the term "Christian" to describe such activities—such as Christian mathematics or Christian landscaping— seems more confusing than helpful.

Education

The first specific topic to consider in this chapter is education. Perhaps no concrete issue explored in this book (at least until we get to politics later in the chapter) is as potentially controversial. Education is obviously a crucial matter for the well-being of both the church and the broader society, and the almost undeniable decline of Western education in previous decades has prompted increasing concern about the issue. Many Christians have invested huge amounts of time and energy into developing Christian schools and colleges and, especially in the past generation, fostering the home-schooling movement. In some churches certain educational practices have become a virtual test of orthodoxy. Does the two-kingdoms doctrine provide any helpful guidance? In this section I discuss what education is and who is responsible for it, whether there is Christian scholarship and a Christian view of various academic disciplines, and how parents should wrestle through questions about home versus Christian versus public education for their children. The two-kingdoms doctrine itself does not tell us everything there is to know about these subjects, but it does provide a useful perspective for coming to understand them better.

Before addressing these three specific topics, however, a few general words about learning are appropriate. While only a small percentage of Christians are scholars or labor in professions that involve intense intellectual work, learning is a task for all Christians. Human intellect is a gift of God, one of the chief things that distinguishes us from other animals, and an important aspect of the image of God. Broadly speaking, therefore, learning is simply a *human* endeavor. But Scripture also emphasizes the special interest that Christians should have in thinking well. The redeemed believer "is being renewed in *knowledge* after the image of its creator" (Col. 3:10). Paul warns us against being conformed to this world and commands us to "be transformed by the renewal of your mind . . ." (Rom. 12:2). We should not be taken "captive by philosophy and empty deceit" (Col. 2:8) but should "destroy arguments and every lofty opinion raised against the knowledge of God, and take every thought captive to obey Christ" (2 Cor. 10:5). In the Old Testament Solomon displayed his wisdom as he "spoke of trees, from the cedar that is in Lebanon to the hyssop that grows out of the wall" and "of beasts, and of birds, and of reptiles, and of fish" (1 Kings 4:33). God is honored when we explore and understand the marvelous world that he has made. Whatever their disagreements on schools and scholarship, Christians should certainly be able to agree about this.

What Is Education, and Who Is Responsible for It?

Discussions about education often proceed without carefully considering basic questions about the very nature of education and who has the authority to dispense it. Nevertheless it is difficult to think clearly about scholarship and home versus Christian versus public schooling without developing some well-formed judgments about these arduous, but important, preliminary issues.

A first question is, what is education itself? Critics of modern educational trends often complain about the fragmentation of knowledge. Teachers convey individual skills or facts but pay little attention to the coherence of knowledge or to the student as a person. In contrast, advocates of traditional forms of education call for *holistic* learning. For them, education should seek to train the whole person, creating individuals of virtue and not simply brains crammed

173

with facts or future workers with vocational skills.[3] Furthermore, they believe that education should teach students not simply to know individual facts or disciplines but to understand the world of facts and disciplines in their overarching unity and relation to one another. As John Henry Newman said famously from a Roman Catholic perspective, a university should be a place of teaching "universal knowledge."[4] Or, in the terminology of some Christian writers, teachers should teach individual facts and disciplines as parts of a larger "world and life view."

Contemporary Christians can hardly help but be sympathetic to these critiques of much that passes for "education" in contemporary society. But the question of what education is requires that we also inquire about the nature of the various fields of learning and about who ought to be educating. What we should expect teachers to be doing for students—conveying facts, or shaping virtue, or communicating a worldview, or all of the above—depends upon what various academic disciplines (e.g., history or chemistry) are and what authority teachers and institutions possess. The two-kingdoms doctrine offers helpful guidelines.

First, then, what is the nature of the various academic disciplines and what relation do they bear to the two kingdoms? One discipline, theology, stands out from all the rest because its primary concern is to interpret and explain special revelation as found in the Scriptures (though secondarily, in order to aid its interpretation of Scripture, it relies upon natural revelation, as interpreted by other academic disciplines such as linguistics and geography). The primary concern of all other disciplines—whether in the humanities, social sciences, or natural sciences—is to interpret and explain natural revelation, that is, the truth revealed in creation, as upheld and governed by God through the Noahic covenant (Ps. 19:1–6; Rom. 1:19–20; 2:14–15). These disciplines seek not to exegete Scripture but to understand, for example, literature, the human economic order, or biological

---

[3]For example, this is a theme running through C. S. Lewis's classic work, *The Abolition of Man* (New York: Macmillan, 1947).

[4]John Henry Cardinal Newman, *The Idea of a University* (reprinted, Westminster, MD: Christian Classics, 1982), ix.

processes. Though these disciplines focus upon interpreting natural revelation, however, Scripture says significant things relevant for them all. Each field of learning explores some aspect of the created order, and thus the very first thing taught in Scripture, that God has created all things, pertains generally to all academic inquiry. God's upholding the natural order (Gen. 8:21–22) underlies mathematics and the natural sciences, his upholding the social order (Gen. 9:1–7) underlies the social sciences, and the twin facts of human sinfulness and image-bearing (Gen. 1:26–27; 3:16–19; 9:6) underlie the humanities.

These considerations suggest that Scripture says crucial things about *the big picture* of all the academic disciplines, while it is silent about nearly all the *narrower, technical details* of these disciplines (except theology). (I recognize that this can only be a general rule and that it will not always be clear where to draw the line between the big picture and the technical details.) Scripture teaches that God upholds the order of nature, but it does not explain trigonometry or how to play the oboe. Only examination and experimentation with the natural order itself can yield such knowledge.

How do the various academic disciplines relate to the two kingdoms? As argued in chapter 6, the church, through her ministry, is to instruct the people of God in all the things that Scripture says: "devote yourself to the public reading of Scripture, to exhortation, to *teaching*" (1 Tim. 4:13); it must declare "the whole counsel of God" (Acts 20:27). This indicates, first of all, that the discipline of theology, whose primary purpose is to interpret and communicate the Scriptures, is under the primary jurisdiction of the church.[5] The church must teach the theological truths of Scripture. Second, the church must also teach ideas that have broad relevance for all the academic disciplines, that is, the big-picture concerns about which Scripture speaks. Since the church is to proclaim *all* that the

---

[5]To clarify, this does not mean that parents, teachers, and professors cannot teach theology in other contexts. It does mean, I believe, that those who teach theology are accountable to the church for their theological views and that there must be a clear distinction between ordained ministers who teach the Scriptures with the authority of Christ and those who teach theology without this office and authority. I touch upon these issues again in the next paragraph with respect to parents' authority to teach their children.

Scriptures say, then the church should teach something (directly or indirectly) about every discipline. Third, the obligation of the church to proclaim *only* what the Scriptures say, and no more, means that the church and her ministers have no authority from Christ to teach the technical details of the nontheological disciplines. Since the primary concern of these academic disciplines is to interpret natural revelation, not Scripture, these disciplines themselves are not under the church's jurisdiction. The chief and primary educational responsibility in these other fields of learning, therefore, resides in the common kingdom.

Within the common kingdom the family is of first and foremost importance when it comes to education. Scripture indicates that God has entrusted parents with the primary responsibility for raising and training their own children (e.g., Prov. 1:8–9). Though the state, business corporations, and other common kingdom institutions have great interest in an educated populace, primary jurisdiction for childhood education resides within the family. Based upon previous discussion, I would clarify this point by saying that parents have primary authority for educating their children in the nontheological academic disciplines, but only *secondary* jurisdiction for educating them in theology (and in whatever else Scripture teaches). Christ entrusted the keys of the kingdom of heaven to the church (Matt. 16:18–19), gave pastors and teachers to the church for attaining "to the unity of the faith and of the knowledge of the Son of God . . ." (Eph. 4:13; see vv. 7–16), and commissioned the church's ministry with the task of guarding the flock through the Word of God (Acts 20:27–28). God has commanded Christian parents to reinforce the church's biblical teaching in the home (Prov. 22:6; Eph. 6:4), a command that parents seldom take seriously enough. But they should undertake their children's biblical and theological education ultimately under the authority of their church's ministers and elders.

As stated above, however, parents have primary jurisdiction over their children's education in nontheological fields of learning. They have every right to assert this authority if the state or other institutions encroach upon it. At the same time, Christians have ordinarily recognized that parents may delegate their authority to others to aid them in the education of their children. Parents have various limitations with respect to knowledge, pedagogical skill, time, and resources, and they may entrust aspects of their children's education to other people. In this concept lies the origin of schools. We will return to this issue below when we consider matters concerning home, Christian, and public education.

These considerations about jurisdiction and authority permit us to return to questions about the holistic training of children. As noted, many critics of modern education lament its failure to train the whole person and to convey a sense of universal, integrated knowledge in the context of a world and life view. Christian theology gives many reasons to appreciate such critiques of modern education: one God upholds the world and gives it order and meaning, truth does exist and it may be known, and human intellect and morality are designed to work in tandem. These are excellent principles to guide Christian teachers in their work, as they strive for coherence between their big-picture convictions and the technical aspects of their discipline. At the same time, Christian theology—and the two-kingdoms doctrine in particular—also provides reasons to be cautious and modest about attempts to provide holistic education. Neither the church nor the family (nor the school to which parents delegate authority) has competence to impart a comprehensively detailed world and life view.

This is true for the church, on the one hand, because it has authority to shape the whole person and provide a view of the whole, but has no authority to teach how exactly this should work out in the various fields of learning. The power of the Word and sacraments in the church instill true virtue in a human being and provide the fullness of knowledge about God and the purposes and destiny of this world. As considered above, the church must say many things that have broad relevance for all fields of human learning, but cannot teach the technical details of these other disciplines. Parents and schools, on the other hand, have authority to explore and to teach the technical details of these disciplines, but do not have an authoritative office to interpret and minister God's Word in the name of Christ. Christian parents should be teaching their children the Bible as they reinforce the church's biblical education, but even parents have no right to *preach* the Word or to administer the sacraments, which are God's specially ordained ways to make his people grow in grace. Attempts by parents and schoolteachers to show how the minutiae of academics fit into the whole truth of Scripture must be suggestive and provisional rather than definitive.

In light of these various limitations, we do well to be humble in our claims about holistic education and modest in our expectations from ourselves, our churches, and our schools. Diligent parents, pastors, and teachers can all, in their own ways, point students' thinking in holistic directions. Yet we are sojourners and exiles, those who in the present age "walk by faith, not by sight" (2 Cor. 5:7) and who "now . . . see in a mirror dimly . . ." (1 Cor. 13:12). No institution in the present world, of either the redemptive kingdom or the common kingdom, has the authority or competence to communicate a holistic, all-encompassing, and fully integrated world and life view.

Though we will consider different sorts of schooling options below, a few remarks concerning Christian schools seem appropriate here. In light of the jurisdiction that Christ has given to his church to minister the Word and sacraments and the jurisdiction he has given to the church's officers to oversee Christians' spiritual well-being, Christian schools should be mindful not to usurp the church's responsibilities as their own. Many Christian schools devote significant time to service/mission projects, chapel and prayer services, and spiritual emphasis weeks. It is worthwhile for administrators and teachers to ponder why their schools would spend time on such things. Do they believe that Christ has insufficiently equipped his church for missions, worship, and the spiritual growth of her members? Have they done a fully sufficient job of teaching reading, mathematics, and science, such that they have extra time to pursue these other activities? As ministers should hesitate to instruct about mathematics from the pulpit, so mathematics teachers should hesitate to instruct about missions and prayer in their schools. Both ministers in the pulpit and teachers in the classroom should give careful thought to what they teach and should strive to educate with excellence within the proper bounds that God has given them.[6]

Christian Disciplines and Christian Scholarship

Another difficult and controversial subject related to education is whether to attach the adjective "Christian" to nontheological fields of learning and scholarship. What people mean when they use "Christian" in this way (or refuse to do so) is not always clear. Though the two-kingdoms doctrine is not designed to resolve every particular question that arises in this regard, it again offers some helpful perspective as each Christian (and especially each Christian teacher or professor) thinks through the issue.

As discussed above, Scripture says things relevant to every field of learning. Insofar as Scripture speaks, it speaks truly, and Christians are obligated to pursue their academic inquiries and teaching within the bounds that Scripture draws. Christian scholars and teachers may never pursue their work independent of or divorced from their Christian faith. *Study and teaching are never religiously neutral.* In this sense we can speak of a general Christian view of the various academic disciplines.

As also considered above, Scripture does not address the narrower, technical details of these various academic disciplines, which are learned through the study of natural revelation. This has important bearings on the "Christian" character of teaching and scholarship. Teaching and learning the natural sciences, social sciences, and humanities concern the world that God temporarily upholds through the Noahic covenant of Genesis 9, and thus are activities of the *common kingdom*. This implies that they are joint activities of believers and unbelievers. Teaching and studying physics, economics, and French literature are *human* activities for which Christians can claim no special propriety. Christians who pursue these disci-

---

[6]A recent book that makes a thoughtful and winsome case that Christian schools (especially at the university level) should be worshiping communities and extensions of the church is James K. A. Smith's *Desiring the Kingdom: Worship, Worldview, and Cultural Formation* (Grand Rapids: Baker, 2009). Smith offers helpful discussion of many issues pertaining to Christianity and culture, though I believe that a biblical two-kingdoms doctrine stands contrary to this kind of blending of church and school.

plines must abide within the boundaries of biblical teaching. They must always avoid *anti-Christian* views of each discipline. They cannot study physics under the assumption that there is no Creator who upholds order in the universe, or study history with materialistic assumptions. But the fact that pursuing these disciplines are activities of the common kingdom indicates that believers should be cautious and modest about claiming their academic work and conclusions as "Christian."

One reason for this caution is the fact that natural revelation, upon which these academic disciplines are based, comes to all human beings equally under the Noahic covenant, and all human beings are equally bound to submit to its truth. In contrast to the special revelation of Scripture, which has been entrusted to the church and gives many moral exhortations aimed distinctively at those already united to Christ, God imparts natural revelation to all without distinction (though even here Christians have the great advantage of having Scripture to *clarify* what natural revelation teaches). The truths of natural revelation that Christians discover when investigating physics, economics, or French literature are truths that are also accessible to unbelievers and oftentimes acknowledged by them too—and frequently discovered by them first.

A second reason for this caution is that one Christian's technical theories and interpretations of natural revelation in a given academic discipline should not be imposed upon another Christian. Christian scholars have liberty to develop theories about physics, economics, or French literature, but they cannot demand that other Christians accept their views as *the Christian* theory. The difficulty with one scholar's claim to have developed or discovered the "Christian" approach to physics, economics, or French literature is that another Christian may rightfully come along and, within the same boundaries of biblical teaching, develop a competing approach.

Though I caution against overly zealous attempts to label one's own approach to an academic discipline as "Christian," Christian teachers and scholars must always be vigilant about how people's basic presuppositions can distort their study and teaching. Even the narrower, technical aspects of academic disciplines are liable to perversion by sinful human beings (Christians as well as non-Christians). Since sin is pervasive in human nature, sin will be pervasive in human activities. Yet while Christians are in fundamental conflict with unbelievers in regard to their basic presuppositions about God and the world (the *antithesis*), they find that they can often cooperate with them on a great many things when it comes to the narrower and technical aspects of their work. Biblical teaching about the Noahic covenant and the common kingdom explains why this is true. Unbelievers must live in this world and, under God's providential common grace, the necessities of life often constrain them from denying basic facts about how the world works and how individuals and society operate. Believers have the obligation, under the terms of the Noahic covenant, to cooperate as much as possible with unbelieving practitioners of their discipline. Indeed, why would we not want to acknowledge the many scientific, musical, literary, and other gifts that God has given to unbelievers and learn what we can from their achievements?

What bearing do these reflections have on the question of "Christian scholarship" that George Marsden, most prominently, has probed in recent years? Insofar as Christians explore the big-picture biblical boundaries of their disciplines, the effect of basic religious presuppositions on the study and teaching of their fields, and the basic faith-driven motivations for pursuing them, the idea of "Christian scholarship" is a useful concept. These are meaningful subjects that believers must explore from a uniquely Christian perspective.

The idea of "Christian scholarship" seems less useful, however, with regard to the technical research and teaching of these disciplines. For one thing, technical research and teaching depend upon the exploration of natural revelation, which believers cannot claim as their exclusive possession, since it is accessible to all alike in the common kingdom under the Noahic covenant. It seems reasonable to assume, nevertheless, that Christian scholars will encounter the distorting effects of non-Christian presuppositions upon technical work in certain academic fields more often than in other fields. I suggest (without presuming to know with certainty) that these effects might be felt more intensely in the humanities, which deal more directly and regularly with the evaluation of human conduct and the interpretation of life's meaning than do, for instance, the natural sciences.[7] It is interesting, however, that many writers in both the humanities and natural sciences, when identifying what is distinctively Christian about believing scholars' work, do an excellent job of showing the distinctiveness of their big-picture ideas and subjective motivation but provide little about how their technical research and teaching is distinctively Christian. Marsden, a historian, offers one example. All four of his illustrations of how faith has a bearing on scholarship focus on big-picture issues or motivation, and none on the actual technical practice of the disciplines themselves.[8] The same is true for a recent book on Christian pursuit of the natural sciences by two Christian college professors, Tim Morris and Don Petcher. These authors offer very helpful discussions about a broad Christian perspective on the natural world. But even their most specific applications of this broad perspective remain at a very general level. Most of their applications are neither uniquely Christian nor even unique to the natural sciences.[9] These thoughtful books, I believe, indirectly lend credence to my suggestion that we should be cautious and modest about using the term "Christian" to describe our technical study and teaching of an academic discipline.

What Kind of Schools for Our Children?

To conclude this section I now raise perhaps the most controversial subject among Christians with respect to learning: where should we educate our children? To keep this discussion within manageable bounds I will be thinking predominantly about primary and secondary education (not college and beyond), and I will focus upon the three options that ordinarily receive the most attention,

---

[7] A similar point is suggested by George M. Marsden in *The Outrageous Idea of Christian Scholarship* (New York: Oxford University Press, 1997), 63.

[8] See Marsden, *The Outrageous Idea*, 63–64. Marsden himself had commented earlier (61): "Everyone recognizes that the differences will not be apparent in the technical dimensions of their work, but that implications of the faith may sometimes have an important bearing on their theories and interpretations."

[9] E.g., see Tim Morris and Don Petcher, *Science & Grace: God's Reign in the Natural Sciences* (Wheaton: Crossway, 2006), 240–42, 252–78, 301–6.

homeschools, Christian schools, and public schools. Of course, the existence of private schools that are not specifically Christian and the advent of public charter schools, which in some cases employ many Christian teachers and use a classical curriculum, make this issue even more complicated. The two-kingdoms doctrine, I conclude, suggests that where to educate our children is a decision that must be left to the liberty of each Christian family and that all parents, whatever decision they make, must be vigilant about their children's education and attentive to the shortcomings of every educational option.

First, the question of how believing parents should educate their children is a matter of Christian liberty. The church, as the present earthly manifestation of the redemptive kingdom, has authority to teach the whole of the Scriptures and nothing beyond. The Bible does not offer clear instruction about method of schooling (in fact, it does not talk about schools at all), and thus there is no single required Christian option. Parents have a unique authority in the common kingdom to supervise their children's education, and Christians may not impose their own judgments upon the consciences of other Christians. At the same time, churches ought to be concerned about the decisions that parents make, for such decisions can have significant implications for children's spiritual development. Pastors and elders should encourage parents to take educational decisions very seriously and should help them think through issues in a wise way, without imposing a particular choice or manipulating consciences. Churches without controversies about education should take care that parents do not become indifferent about the subject, while churches that are tempted to impose a single way, whether directly or indirectly, should take care not to trample upon others' consciences through extrabiblical opinions.

Christian sojourners participating in two kingdoms have multiple concerns to think about in this area. In light of their unique Christian convictions they will be concerned about the broad perspective and biases with which academic subjects are addressed. They will also be concerned about the technical ability of teachers to inspire, discipline, and communicate knowledge about their fields—abilities possessed by many non-Christian teachers, often to a greater degree than their Christian counterparts. Among the chief concerns of parents in choosing educational options for their children, therefore, will be the teachers' knowledge of the subjects they teach, the teachers' pedagogical abilities, the teachers' ability to maintain an orderly and disciplined classroom environment, the quality of the fellow students with whom their children will learn, and the broader perspectives and biases of the teachers (and of fellow students). Some Christian parents may find that a particular available schooling option is superior to other options at all of these points and that their decision is an easy one. Many Christian parents, however, find that different options available to them present various advantages and disadvantages with respect to these concerns (not to mention other potential issues such as financial costs).

Parents weighing their options do well to avoid erring in either of two directions. First, parents should not think that a teacher's or school's religious presuppositions do not affect matters such as curriculum, learning environment, and pedagogical method. The effects can be subtle or overt, but the deceitfulness of sin is never to be underestimated and parents must be vigilant about its propensity to corrupt. Though this is of special concern with regard to unbelieving teachers, many professing Christian teachers also work with presuppositions at odds with Christian truth, with deleterious effects on their pedagogy. Second, parents should not assume that simply because a teacher has a sound religious commitment, he is therefore a more competent teacher or scholar than an unbeliever. Non-Christians often have made greater contributions to human learning than Christians have. If we love God's world and take the Noahic covenant seriously, we should wish to learn from unbelievers whom God has enabled to understand wonderful things about his creation and to communicate them to others. We impoverish our children educationally if we unduly cut them off from the accomplishments and contributions of unbelievers.

When parents consider the various criteria they should use to make choices about their children's education, they may feel that different options provide different advantages and drawbacks. This could be, in fact, a healthy feeling. A hidden danger is that parents sometimes do not recognize the limitations of the educational option they have chosen for their children and therefore do nothing to compensate or correct for its limitations. There is no perfect school or homeschool. Homeschool parents should beware of overestimating their own abilities to provide a full and rich education for their children without outside help, and parents who send their children to school should beware of ceding all interest in their children's education, as if schools can do it all. Parents should not, I suggest, choose any one educational option to the exclusion of all the others.

Homeschooling offers the obvious advantage of giving parents immediate control over presuppositions, curricula, discipline, and overall learning environment. Given the state of so many schools today, this is no small advantage. At the same time, simply because parents have control over these things does not mean that they are learned and have good pedagogical skills. Many well-meaning people, talented in other areas, are simply not effective teachers. Other parents are indeed competent teachers, and those who have the desire and opportunity might pursue the homeschool option. Even well-educated and pedagogically competent parents, however, are surely not more competent than all other teachers in all subjects at every grade level. And the home, however conducive an environment for learning in many ways, is limited in the range of experiences and opportunities that it can provide children as they grow and mature. Thus in order to ensure that their children learn how to deal with different kinds of people, gain skills and knowledge that their parents lack, and come to understand the broader world, homeschooling parents should probably make use of other teachers and learning environments at various points in their children's education.

Sending children to Christian schools means that parents give up a certain degree of control over the perspective from which material is taught, as well as over curricula, discipline, and overall learning environment. One of the ideas behind a *Christian* school, however, is that parents should have a significant degree of trust in the biases of teachers, administrators, and even their children's classmates. By

185

choosing this option, parents hope to gain access to teachers who have more knowledge and/or pedagogical ability than they themselves do and hope to provide their children with a broader exposure to social situations and the wider world than they alone can provide in the home. But just because a teacher is a professing Christian does not guarantee that her presuppositions are those of the parents or that she has excellent knowledge of the subject and pedagogical and disciplinary skills. Nor are classmates at the Christian school always wholesome friends and learning companions. Parents must monitor what their children are learning even in Christian schools and seek to supplement what is inevitably lacking in their curricula—no school can teach a child everything there is to know. The controlled environment of a Christian school also limits students' exposure to non-Christian adults and children. Understanding how to interact with and learn from unbelievers is an important part of living in this world, and thus parents of Christian school students probably do well to seek opportunities for their children to participate in secular learning environments. Daniel would likely have been a less effective servant of the Babylonian court had he not received some Babylonian education (Dan. 1:3–4, 17–21).

Public schools perhaps present the most difficult challenges to Christian parents, due not only to the non-Christian biases of pedagogy and curricula but also to the general dumbing-down of educational standards and decline in disciplinary demands in recent generations (I speak from an American perspective). Nevertheless, as some Christian parents discover, there are still many excellent teachers and fine learning opportunities in public schools. With the advent of charter schools, furthermore, there are now "public" schools staffed largely by people with Christian sentiments or others with high educational standards. Some Christian parents simply do not have viable options for homeschooling or Christian schools, even if they consider these ideal, and will have to make the best of their public school option(s). They will have to be especially vigilant about guarding their children against anti-Christian biases and supplementing the shortcomings in public education with other wholesome educational opportunities. But such parents may also be most immune from the temptation to think that a school can provide a perfect and holistic education for their children and from the danger of looking to a school to do what only the church can and should do. Sometimes parents may find it easier to guard their children against big and obvious lies perpetrated in a public school than against subtle lies that may be communicated even in a Christian school.

Vocation

By "vocation" I refer to what we usually call our work, occupation, or profession. Vocation usually refers to what we do for a living—that is, for our financial well-being—but this is not always the case. For example, many people legitimately claim full-time parenting or full-time homemaking as their vocation without drawing any salary for their work. Whether paid or unpaid, work must be productive to constitute a vocation. Spending each day watching television or playing a daily round of recreational golf are not vocations in the sense that gainful employment or rearing a family are. The term "vocation," furthermore, indicates that our work is a *calling*. God is the one who ultimately calls each person to productive work and grants that work, however mundane, a noble character.

The topic of vocation does not usually garner the same controversies and tensions among Christians that education and politics do. Nevertheless, their vocations occupy a great deal of most Christians' lives and tend to define their existence in ways that transcend the workplace. Christians struggle with what vocations to choose or abandon, how to balance work demands with life's other demands, and whether there are distinctively Christian ways to perform their vocations. Though I cannot address all of these issues in detail, I suggest that the two-kingdoms doctrine again offers much helpful perspective for thinking through them.

An initial point, which previous chapters have anticipated, is that productive labor is ordained by God and inherently dignified. As many of the Protestant Reformers rightly emphasized, our conscientious work is honorable and God-glorifying whether we grind away at menial jobs, labor in the halls of power, or preach the gospel from the pulpit. All work that is lawful and beneficial has his blessing. God made human beings in his image for the purpose of exercising dominion in this world. God exerted his labor upon this world in bringing it into existence and giving it order, and from the beginning he called his human creatures to exert their labor upon it under his authority (Gen. 1:26–28). After the fall into sin God revealed that human labor would lie under a curse and thus be subject to pain and frustration (Gen. 3:17–19). Work often seems vain and fails to satisfy (Eccles. 1:2–3; 6:7). Yet God's words after the fall also meant that fallen human beings would remain working creatures, and they produced wonderful cultural artifacts (Gen. 4:20–22). In the Noahic covenant God reaffirmed that all human beings bear his image, albeit in a fallen and corrupted way, and thus would continue to pursue various vocational tasks (Gen. 9:1–7).

Human work after the fall, therefore, ordinarily belongs to the *common kingdom* (with some important exceptions). Ancient and venerable vocations such as farming, making music, and metallurgy belonged not to believers alone but to believers and unbelievers in common. Jabal, Jubal, and Tubal-Cain, from the unbelieving line of Cain, excelled in them (Gen. 4:20–22). Rearing children and doing justice also belonged to the human race generally (Gen. 9:1–7). Believers are always citizens of the redemptive kingdom and must pursue all of their labors in a way consistent with this identity. They should perform every task out of faith in Christ (Rom. 14:23; Heb. 11:6) and for his glory (1 Cor. 10:31). As they pursue their daily vocations in this way, God calls most of them to work in businesses and organizations that are institutions of the common kingdom. Though the church benefits in many ways when such institutions function well, contributions to these institutions, even when performed by Christians, do not build the redemptive kingdom as such. The redemptive kingdom is built through the church's ministry of the Word, the sacraments, prayer, and discipline.

In my judgment, this observation suggests that Christian writers should mitigate some of the sweeping language often used when describing work. Many authors speak about the Christian's vocation as "holy" or "sacred" and claim that God "redeems" it. But while

Christians themselves are holy and redeemed, as citizens of the redemptive kingdom, their daily vocations are not. They labor in the things of *this present world*, things that are transient and fleeting. Many of the writers who speak of the Christian's vocation in "holy" or "redemptive" categories make true and important points that should be widely acknowledged: work of all sorts is intrinsically valuable, meaningful, and God-honoring.[10] Our vocations have this character, however, not because the businesses we run or the products we make or our modest contributions to world economic growth are building the new heaven and new earth (or because they open up opportunities for evangelism, though this can be a wonderful side benefit). Daily labor is inherently good because God is the Creator and sustainer of this good world in which we work. Despite the fall into sin, God blessed the world and human labor within it through the Noahic covenant. God does not promise to Christians that the products of their labor will adorn the New Jerusalem—in fact, Scripture indicates just the opposite—but he does grant them seasons of joy and satisfaction in the midst of mundane toil.

Ecclesiastes is instructive. It makes clear that the work of our hands does not endure (5:15). Yet in the midst of our transitory workplaces God grants joy as a gift of his grace. "There is nothing better for a person than that he should eat and drink and find enjoyment in his toil. This also, I saw, is from the hand of God, for apart from him who can eat or who can have enjoyment?" (2:24–25). "What gain has the worker from his toil? . . . I perceived that there is nothing better for them than to be joyful and to do good as long as they live; also that everyone should eat and drink and take pleasure in all his toil—this is God's gift to man" (3:9, 12–13). The believer finds satisfaction in his work not because it is somehow removed from the confines of this world and made holy or redeemed. Scripture says nothing of such things. The believer finds satisfaction in his vocation because God graciously gives him joy *in the midst of* the confines of this world. Ecclesiastes indicates that Christians who seek satisfaction

---

[10]See e.g., Leland Ryken, *Work & Leisure in Christian Perspective* (Portland: Multnomah, 1987); and David H. Jensen, *Responsive Labor: A Theology of Work* (Louisville: Westminster John Knox, 2006).

in their work by transforming the world or building the redemptive kingdom are looking in the wrong place. Instead we should cry out to God to impart enjoyment in the simple tasks of work itself. Hard work, with God's blessing, is truly its own reward.

One other question related to the terms "holy" and "redeemed" deserves brief mention: what is the relation of the common kingdom vocations, which I had principally in mind in the preceding paragraphs, to ecclesiastical vocations, specifically the gospel ministry but also (often part-time) ecclesiastical vocations such as serving as an elder or deacon? Many writers stress that all work is holy and redeemed because they wish to avoid the idea that so-called "secular" vocations (such as farming or accounting) are inferior to so-called "sacred" vocations (particularly the gospel ministry). This idea should indeed be avoided. The factory worker should not view his work as demeaning, in comparison to that of his pastor. But we must not forget the very important distinction between vocations in the church (the redemptive kingdom) and vocations outside the church (the common kingdom). The gospel ministry in particular is *not* just one profession among many. The Lord Jesus and his apostles never lamented the lack of good engineers or gave instructions for training electricians, but Christ did say, "The harvest is plentiful, but the laborers are few; therefore pray earnestly to the Lord of the harvest to send out laborers into his harvest" (Matt. 9:37-38), and Paul commanded Timothy: "what you have heard from me in the presence of many witnesses entrust to faithful men who will be able to teach others also" (2 Tim. 2:2). Their work of ministering the gospel is what elicits faith in sinners and builds the church as the kingdom of heaven. All vocations are honorable, but "let the elders who rule well be considered worthy of double honor, especially those who labor in preaching and teaching" (1 Tim. 5:17). The church's vocations have their origin in the redemptive kingdom while all other vocations have their origin in creation as divinely upheld through the Noahic covenant. The work of the ministry is truly a holy vocation. To say that other vocations are secular or common is not to insult them, but simply to respect proper biblical distinctions.[11]

What does Scripture say about Christians' conduct in carrying out their common vocations, and is there something distinctively Christian about it? The New Testament gives some general instructions about conduct on the job. Christians should work hard and not be idle (2 Thess. 3:6–12; see also Prov. 6:6–11; 13:4; 19:15; 21:25), should do their work quietly and mind their own business (1 Thess. 4:11–12), and should respect authority structures in the workplace (Col. 3:22–24). Other moral commands in Scripture—such as kindness, honesty, and justice—are widely applicable in our vocations as well, but this is about all that the New Testament specifically says about vocational ethics.

What does this mean for the question of whether there is a "Christian" way of doing our work? Can we and should we speak of Christian plumbing or Christian lawyering? Such language can be helpful in certain senses. It is highly fitting, for example, to attach the adjective "Christian" to believers' labor in terms of their *subjective* attitude and motivation. Unbelievers may have all sorts of motivations for pursuing their vocations, but Christians are to pursue theirs "in Christ" (see 2 Thess. 3:12). Their work should reflect their faith in him and should be dedicated to his glory. They must be on guard against letting the wisdom of this world skew their perspective on work. They should sweat over their daily toil "under the sun" (Eccles. 2:18) with joyful realization that they have an eternal inheritance that far transcends what is under the sun. None of these things could possibly be true of the unbeliever. The subjective attitude and motivation of the Christian worker should be radically different from that of her non-Christian colleague.

The ordinary work of believers also has a distinctively Christian flavor insofar as doing their work well will "adorn the doctrine of God our Savior" (Titus 2:10). In a world in which sin pervades the

---

[11]One potentially difficult question that the preceding paragraphs raise is how to evaluate vocations in so-called "parachurch" organizations, which are not the church itself but seek to perform distinctively Christian tasks in order to assist the church. Due to constraints of space I will leave this question for readers to contemplate and hope to address it myself at a later date.

workplace, basic things like maintaining one's integrity, using sound speech, and not stealing provide testimony to the reality of God's grace and the power of the gospel (Titus 2:4–10).

In other ways, however, the adjective "Christian" is less helpful and accurate when describing the believer's vocation. First, the Christian's attitude and motivation toward labor and Scripture's commands about conduct in the workplace are of a general nature. They are not specific to any particular vocation. The Christian obligation to work as an expression of faith and for the glory of God applies equally to the physician, the homemaker, and the carpenter. The biblical commands to be industrious, to mind one's own business, and to respect authority on the job apply equally to the dentist and the firefighter. These obligations and commands indicate what should characterize a Christian worker generally, but they offer little to indicate what makes a Christian *physician* distinctive from a Christian *homemaker*. In other words, whatever would describe a "Christian dentist" would work about as well for describing a "Christian firefighter."

Second, using the adjective "Christian" to describe the believer's vocation becomes unhelpful when it obscures the importance of Christian liberty and wisdom. The church has authority to teach all that Scripture teaches but nothing beyond, and in extrabiblical matters Christians must exercise their own wisdom to make God-pleasing decisions. Christians should offer mutual help, encouragement, and wise advice to one another in such things, but they cannot impose *the* Christian decision upon another Christian where Scripture is silent. The vast majority of what most workers do each day involves decisions for which Scripture provides no clear direction. The physician's day is filled with decisions about diagnosing and prescribing medication for her patients. The truck driver's day is filled with decisions about speeding up, slowing down, and changing lanes. The homemaker's day is filled with decisions about her children's eating schedule and whether a dirty toilet or dusty end table needs more urgent attention. Each Christian must seek to make such decisions with care and diligence, but one Christian may disagree with another Christian about his judgments and neither has the right to claim his own as *the* Christian way. To speak about "Christian homemaking" or "Christian truck driving" therefore says little about most of the concrete, objective decisions that believers make on the job each day.

Third, the adjective "Christian" seems unhelpful for describing the believer's vocation insofar as the concrete, objective biblical commands about workplace conduct are not unique to the Christian. Biblical workplace requirements for Christians are also things we rightly expect from unbelievers. Believing lawyers ought to be hardworking and just, but we would demand the same things from an unbelieving lawyer whom we employ. The believing plumber should be honest and environmentally responsible, but we would expect the same from the unbelieving plumber working under our sink. As vocations to which Christians and non-Christians alike are called in the common kingdom, their objective ethics are determined by the moral demands binding all people under the Noahic covenant. Honesty, industriousness, and justice in the workplace are "Christian" obligations in that Christians are obliged to pursue them, but they are not uniquely Christian, since the same demands oblige non-Christians.

Some writers provide (unintentional) confirmation of this point. One writer, advocating a "new creation" model for transforming work, lists its "normative principles" as freedom for all individuals, satisfaction of all people's basic needs, and protection of nature from irreparable damage.[12] Another writer promotes a "contemporary Christian perspective on business," which promotes the principles of fair trading practices for workers, healthy local businesses, and Christian-run start-up businesses that "lovingly serve the needs of fellow citizens."[13] Both sets of principles are admirable, but there is nothing distinctively "new creation" or "Christian" about either of them. All of these principles are grounded in the present created order and the terms of the Noahic covenant. The odds are good, in

---

[12]Miroslav Volf, *Work in the Spirit: Toward a Theology of Work* (Oxford: Oxford University Press, 1991), 194.

[13]Michael W. Goheen and Craig G. Bartholomew, *Living at the Crossroads: An Introduction to Christian Worldview* (Grand Rapids: Baker Academic, 2008), 147–49.

fact, that if you ask your unbelieving neighbor whether he believes in freedom, satisfaction of basic needs, ecological responsibility, fair trade, and healthy local businesses, he will heartily agree.

Likewise, the objective standards of excellence for each vocation are ordinarily not distinctively Christian. When a landscaper converts to Christianity, the standard for a well-maintained garden does not suddenly change. Airline passengers desire the same safe and smooth landing from believing and unbelieving pilots. Christians should have a very different perspective on attaining excellence in their work than non-Christians do, but the objective standards of excellence are common to both.

Politics

Politics arouses passionate opinions and disagreements among Christians. Do Christians have an obligation to be politically active? Should they identify themselves with certain political parties, movements, and candidates that promote the right causes? What political voice, if any, should the church adopt, and what should preachers say about political topics from the pulpit? The two-kingdoms doctrine is immensely helpful for reflecting upon such issues.

While I hope that the following point is evident to those who have read previous chapters, it is worth reemphasizing in the strongest terms: *politics is a matter of the common kingdom*. The activities and institutions of the common kingdom have been ordained by God and are thus legitimate and profitable. Civil governments and civil magistrates exist by God's appointment and with his blessing. Yet it is also important to remember that, like other matters of the common kingdom, these things are temporary, provisional, and passing. In the heat of the political moment, when Christians can get so exercised about the latest news from Washington or feel so jubilant or discouraged about the latest election results, maintaining a proper perspective on politics is crucial. Christians must strive neither to deny the importance of politics—since it has great bearing on the justice, peace, and prosperity of this world—nor to exalt politics as a means for ushering in the redemptive kingdom of heaven. The two-kingdoms doctrine effectively guards against both dangerous extremes.

The latter extreme—exalting politics as a means for ushering in the redemptive kingdom—is probably a greater temptation today for most believers than the temptation to despise politics as insignificant or unworthy of Christians. The so-called Religious Right has received heavy criticism in recent years for its identification of Christian commitment with a particular political party's platform and for its attempt to restore America as a Christian nation through political means. Much of the criticism is well deserved. It is interesting, however, to see many of the harshest Christian critics of the Religious Right conflating politics and the redemptive kingdom no less egregiously. As one such critic puts it, in setting out his own vision in contrast to that of the Religious Right, "The Good News is that in Him, what Isaiah prophesied is even now breaking loose in history. The Kingdom of God is *transformed people living in a transformed society*, and when we preach this message to people in our day, we are preaching the gospel, the Good News. This hope for God's Kingdom on earth has been, since Christ, in the process of being actualized. . . . It is by getting involved in political processes that Christians exercise one significant method of transforming society—so that within it, justice can roll down (Amos 5:24)."[14] However much they might differ on specific questions of public policy and party alignment, many politically active Christians on both the right and the left seem to agree that Christians' political activity is an instrument for transforming the world according to the pattern of Christ's kingdom.

While Christians should desire civil government to promote justice, whatever justice it achieves is the justice of the common kingdom, not of the redemptive kingdom proclaimed by Christ. As considered in chapters 4 and 5, civil government finds its origin in the Noahic covenant of Genesis 9 (already anticipated in Gen. 4:15), when God decreed that justice should be enforced among all people according to the principle of just proportionality. The New

---

[14]Tony Campolo, *Red Letter Christians: A Citizen's Guide to Faith and Politics* (Ventura, CA: Regal, 2008), 33, 35.

Testament confirms the authority of civil magistrates to carry out this task (most notably in Rom.13:1–7). The kingdom that Christ proclaimed is of a radically different character—a kingdom that is *not* to operate according to the principle of proportionate justice that should guide the state (see Matt. 5:38–42).

A prominent critic of the Religious Right provides a good illustration of confusion on this matter when he writes: "I am against the death penalty in principle. We simply should not kill to show we are against killing."[15] This quote appears in a book in which the author repeatedly hails "the biblical vision of social justice" and the teaching of Jesus. But in an extended discussion of capital punishment he does not even mention the one biblical verse that actually speaks directly about capital punishment in the common kingdom: "Whoever sheds the blood of man, by man shall his blood be shed, for God made man in his own image" (Gen. 9:6). It is understandable how a person could read, for example, the Sermon on the Mount out of context and conclude that capital punishment is a bad thing. But the two-kingdoms doctrine helps us to recognize that the Sermon on the Mount concerns the redemptive kingdom that finds present expression in the church and says *nothing* about the obligation of the state to enforce the death penalty. The prophetic visions about justice, peace, and prosperity in the new heaven and new earth cannot be superimposed upon our current political activity. The justice sought in politics is a temporary and provisional justice, finding its origins in the common kingdom of the Noahic covenant. Trying to achieve eschatological justice through political means is bound to skew a proper perspective on politics. Christians properly seek to contribute to the proper functioning of the state, but their political task is not that of redemptively transforming the state.[16]

Scripture teaches a number of important truths about civil government, and these truths define a Christian view of government

---

[15]Jim Wallis, *God's Politics: Why the Right Gets It Wrong and the Left Doesn't Get It* (New York: HarperSanFrancisco, 2005), 303.

[16]The language of transformation and redemption also appears among writers who purposely seek to distinguish themselves from both the Religious Right and their critics on the left such as Campolo and Wallis. E.g., see Tim J. R. Trumper, *Preaching and Politics: Engagement without Compromise* (Eugene: Wipf & Stock, 2009), 4, 10, 31, 43, 54–55, 72.

and politics. Churches are bound to teach these truths, and Christians should conduct their political lives accordingly. I mention five truths in particular.

First, Scripture teaches that civil magistrates have been established by God (Rom. 13:1–2). Civil authority is ultimately of divine origin and not a human creation. Second, these magistrates are primarily responsible for keeping order and enforcing justice in the affairs of this world. They give approval to those who do good and carry out God's vengeance upon the wrongdoer (Rom. 13:3–4). Their standard of justice, as God's agents in the common kingdom, is strict and proportionate: blood for blood (eye for eye, tooth for tooth) (Gen. 9:6). What believers should expect from their magistrates are civil "welfare" (Jer. 29:7) and thus the opportunity to "lead a peaceful and quiet life . . ." (1 Tim. 2:2). Third, Scripture indicates that Christians have many obligations toward these magistrates who govern by God's appointment. Believers should live in submission to them, render them proper honor, pay their taxes, and pray for them (see Jer. 29:7; Matt. 22:15–21; Rom. 13:1–2, 5–7; 1 Tim. 2:1–2; Titus 3:1; 1 Pet. 2:13–17). The clear exception to the obligation to submit is when magistrates command believers to do things contrary to God's will (see Acts 4:19–20). Fourth, Christians may serve in political offices or other government posts as a legitimate and God-pleasing vocation—even when the governments they serve are less than wonderful. God's instructions to the Babylonian exiles remain a basic model for New Testament Christians, and Daniel and his three godly friends honorably served several pagan kings. In the New Testament neither Jesus nor his apostles demanded that military officers, who were employees of the Roman government, give up their jobs when they professed faith in Christ (see Matt. 8:10; Acts 10:1–11:18).

Fifth, the state's authority is *limited*. Because civil government exists by God's appointment, it should not overstep the bounds that God has established. Two boundaries are worth noting. First, since the state is under God's authority it has no right to operate contrary to his moral law. The state cannot and should not attempt to punish every violation of God's law with civil penalties, but it never has authority to promote what is evil. Second, God has appointed other common kingdom institutions in addition to the state, and this puts serious constraints on civil magistrates. The fact that God has established the family, for example, means that civil magistrates may not interfere with the legitimate authority of parents over their children. The state should support and protect the lawful exercise of authority within the family and other institutions and should not usurp that authority for itself. Christians should believe in limited government.

The preceding five points, I believe, constitute a summary of the biblical, Christian view of civil government and political involvement. The church should teach these things in the course of its preaching the Scriptures, and Christians are obligated to conduct themselves according to these norms. Beyond these biblical boundaries, however, it can be unhelpful and misleading to speak of a "Christian" view of the state or politics.

Speaking of "Christian" politics is potentially misleading, first of all, because believers and unbelievers alike may practice politics in the common kingdom. Unbelievers have as much right as believers to vote and to hold office. Christians must engage in politics alongside of unbelievers and are free to make common cause with them on issues of mutual concern. This was the practice of Daniel and his three friends as they participated in Babylonian political life. Before them, Abraham entered into political and judicial relationships with his pagan neighbors in Canaan (Genesis 14; 20; 21:22–34; 23). Believers and unbelievers alike abide under the authority of the Noahic covenant, and even unbelievers know the basic demands of justice by virtue of God's natural revelation (Rom. 1:18–32; 2:14–15). Objectively speaking, political activity is a common task, not a uniquely Christian task.

Speaking of "Christian" political activity can also be misleading since Scripture only speaks at a general level about civil government and political responsibilities. Beyond the five general points that I outlined above, Scripture says nothing specifically about the concrete decisions that Christians must make about voting, party affiliation, details of public policy, or political strategy. These are decisions of moral gravity, but they are not decisions that one Christian can impose upon the conscience of another Christian. Where Scripture is silent, there is no single Christian position. Each believer must seek to apply, with wisdom, biblical teaching that is relevant to political decisions. Certain political actions are clearly inconsistent with the faith, but many possible approaches to voting, supporting parties, forming public policy, and political strategizing are potentially consistent with the Christian faith. In these areas believers enjoy Christian liberty—and responsibility—to exercise their wisdom in "seek[ing] the welfare of the city where I have sent you into exile . . ." (Jer. 29:7).[17]

To claim that Christians might legitimately disagree about public policy is uncontroversial in regard to many matters. Whether a municipality should build a two-lane or a four-lane road through a certain part of town is clearly an issue of wisdom, not biblical precept. Though Christians might disagree about how to prioritize questions of safety, taxes, and congestion when wrestling with this decision it would take uncanny gumption to claim a divine mandate for one's position. The real difficulty arrives when believers consider public policy questions involving moral issues that *are* addressed in Scripture. In the contemporary American context questions about abortion, marriage, and war are among the most contested political issues. Scripture says many things relevant to these topics, so how much liberty do Christians really have when these topics become political controversies? To what extent are there "Christian" positions on political questions such as abortion, such that the church might promote them and one Christian expect another Christian to hold them?

In my judgment, the general rule is that the church must teach—and Christians may hold one another accountable for believing—all that Scripture says about such topics *as moral issues* but should be silent about such topics *as concrete political or public policy issues*. The biblical teaching on these topics clearly has political

---

[17]A helpful recent book, discussing this issue in detail from a perspective similar to mine, is Clarke D. Forsythe, *Politics for the Greatest Good: The Case for Prudence in the Public Square* (Downers Grove: InterVarsity, 2009).

ramifications. In nearly every case when a moral issue becomes a concrete political or public policy issue, however, believers must make discretionary judgments in order to decide how to apply the clear biblical teaching to the particular situation. And whenever the application of biblical teaching is a matter of discretion and not specified by Scripture itself, the church must be silent and Christians may not impose their own discretionary judgments upon the consciences of other Christians.

Perhaps it would be helpful to illustrate by focusing on a particular topic, abortion. First, what is the biblical, Christian view of abortion and, thus, what should the church teach about it? While Scripture never addresses abortion per se, it teaches indirectly that an unborn baby is a human person from its earliest days and thus deserves to be protected from harm.[18] Therefore, in the course of preaching the Scriptures (including texts such as Ex. 21:22–25, Ps. 51:5, and Ps. 139:13–16), the ministers of the church should teach about the dignity of the human embryo and its need for protection. In private counseling situations or disciplinary cases, pastors and elders should present abortion as a sin and deal with people accordingly (which means not merely exhorting pregnant women not to abort but also in love helping needy women care for the children that they do not abort). The Christian view is that abortion is sinful (leaving aside possible exceptions when the mother's life is threatened). If the church is faithfully doing its job—i.e., teaching all that Scripture teaches—then its stance and witness with respect to our so-called "culture of death" should be clear.

But is there a particular Christian view that the church should promote with respect to abortion as a concrete public policy issue? Christians find themselves in the midst of a fallen world in which rape and fornication produce many unwanted pregnancies, in which many people advocate abortion rights, in which politicians, political parties, and judges hold a variety of views on abortion entangled

---

[18]Many helpful discussions of biblical teaching related to the status of the embryo have been written. I offer my own biblical discussion and defense of prenatal human life in David VanDrunen, *Bioethics and the Christian Life: A Guide to Difficult Decision-Making* (Wheaton: Crossway, 2009), chap. 6.

with their views on related issues, and in which many women, if denied access to legal abortion, will obtain abortions on the black market. To be effective in such a world, Christians cannot simply assert that in an ideal world abortion should always and everywhere be illegal. Christians must consider how to live consistently with their conviction about the evil of abortion in a world that is very far from ideal, and this requires judgments that depend upon discernment and wisdom—judgments about which Christians equally committed to Scripture may disagree. While Christians should never promote abortion as a social good, there are many different ways in which they might oppose abortion.

Take voting as an example. Some Christians refuse to vote for any candidate who does not take a clear pro-life position; in light of the gravity of the abortion issue such a position is understandable. Other Christians decide that they can vote for a pro-choice candidate; perhaps there is no viable pro-life candidate on the ballot, or perhaps the pro-choice candidate holds better views than the pro-life candidate on a great number of other issues (no candidate being perfect), or perhaps abortion policy is unlikely to be affected one way or another by whomever is elected, due to particular political circumstances. Deciding for whom to vote is a serious and morally weighty question, but Scripture itself does not decide it. Two Christians with equal commitment to biblical teaching about abortion may evaluate political circumstances differently and make different discretionary judgments about what will serve the long-term good of society. Their different judgments may not be equally wise, but Scripture itself cannot referee between them. Thus the church may not promote one side over the other nor may any Christian present his decision as the *Christian* view.

Or we might consider the Christian who serves as a state legislator. What should she do if a bill is presented to the legislature that would reduce the availability of abortions in comparison to current practice but would still permit some abortions? Again, two different Christians might share identical views about the evil of abortion but disagree about this bill. One might oppose the bill, reasoning that it would uphold the legality of a terrible action. The other might support the bill, reasoning that it would reduce the frequency of this terrible action, which is the best that can be achieved in the present cultural climate. An important and morally weighty decision, to be sure, but it is one of discretion and wisdom that the minister, bound to preach the Scriptures and the Scriptures alone, cannot determine from the pulpit.

Or we might consider matters of broader political strategy. What is the best way to bring about long-term change in civil law concerning abortion? Some Christians may devote themselves to political activism, perhaps by seeking to shape a political party's abortion position. Others might write law review articles, hoping to turn judicial opinion, in light of the important role that courts have played in determining abortion law (in the American context). Others might conclude that political and judicial activism over the past decades has produced scant results, and thus decide to focus their attention on grassroots cultural attitudes instead, perhaps by writing op-ed pieces or by picketing abortion clinics in order to raise awareness about the issues. Others might leave aside attempts to change broader social forces and focus upon individual cases, volunteering at a crisis pregnancy center and thereby seeking to encourage alternatives to abortion one woman at a time. (Many Christians, because they devote themselves to other important causes in the church and society, might participate in none of these activities.) In each case Christians could make good arguments for the effectiveness of their own strategy, and in some cases could make credible arguments for the ineffectiveness of others' strategies. But no one can demand, as a distinctively Christian obligation, that another believer adopt his strategy and participate in the activities that he judges to be most important.

What final conclusion can be drawn from this case study of abortion? I believe that this case study illustrates that even when a moral issue may be quite clear biblically, individual Christians' attempts to live consistently with biblical teaching in concrete areas of politics and public policy remain matters of discretion and wisdom for which there is no single Christian approach that the church can impose upon the conscience of believers. Churches and their ministers violate this principle frequently. The Roman Catholic Church offers numerous examples. Pope Paul VI, for instance, in a 1965 New York address, formally endorsed the creation and work of the United Nations as a good means for advancing civilization and peace in the world.[19] More recently, Pope Benedict XVI has called for a Palestinian state to help overcome the Middle East crisis and for international bodies to regulate financial markets.[20] Perhaps the United Nations, a two-state solution for Palestine, and international financial regulation are good ideas. But perhaps not. All Christians would agree that promoting civilization and peace are proper goals for political activity, but whether the existence of the United Nations and an independent Palestinian state actually serves these goals is a matter of political judgment about which Christians may disagree, and thus about which church officers, speaking in their official capacities, should not opine. The preacher has no business, "as part of his calling, to be something of a political analyst."[21]

Are there exceptions? Are there times when the resolution of a particular political controversy or public policy debate is so obvious that the church can and must speak about it in the course of its ministry of the Word of God? I cannot foreclose that as a possibility. Each preacher must wrestle conscientiously with the particular text he is expounding and determine what obligations it undoubtedly places upon his hearers.

Conclusion

In this chapter I have sought to put the biblical two-kingdoms doctrine to work by reflecting upon specific areas of the Christian's cul-

---

[19]John O'Malley makes the following comments about this address in *What Happened at Vatican II* (Cambridge, MA: Belknap Press of Harvard University Press, 2008), 262–63: "He then made his first point: he wanted his presence and message to be 'a moral and solemn ratification' of the UN, which he and his immediate predecessors were convinced 'represented the road we must travel in the interests of modern civilization and world peace.' The point he drove home throughout the speech was the imperative for nations to cooperate with one another for the common good of humanity. That was the high vocation and mission to which the United Nations was called."

[20]As the *Wall Street Journal* noted on the front page of its May 12, 2009 edition, the pope "called for Israelis and Palestinians to reach a compromise on a two-state solution." For his statements on regulation of financial markets, see his July 2009 encyclical *Caritas in Veritate*.

[21]Contra the claim of Trumper, *Preaching and Politics*, 13.

tural life. I have argued throughout this book that the two-kingdoms doctrine captures two crucial aspects of biblical teaching. On the one hand, cultural activities and institutions exist by God's appointment and under his moral government, and Christians should participate in them. On the other hand, these cultural activities and institutions should not be confused with the redemptive kingdom of heaven, which finds its present expression in the church of Jesus Christ. Thus we have considered the implications of this general perspective for three important areas of culture. Christians should embrace learning, pursue vocations, and participate in political processes as tasks ordained of God. Scripture says significant things about all of these activities, and Christians are bound to be faithful to biblical teaching as they pursue them. At the same time, due to God's covenant with Noah, Christians generally should pursue them as *common* activities rather than as uniquely *Christian* activities. They should acknowledge the common objective standards of morality and excellence in cultural life that obligate all people. They should cooperate with unbelievers as far as possible for the sake of the temporal good of this fleeting world.

As we come to the end of the book, it may be helpful to put this chapter in broad perspective. From the beginning, God willed that human beings should attain life in the world-to-come through their cultural labors. The first Adam, the original representative of the human race, failed to offer perfect obedience to God in his cultural task and plunged the world into sin and misery. But God sent the second and last Adam, the Lord Jesus Christ, to atone for the sin of the first Adam and to accomplish his task. Christ has rendered perfect obedience to God in every area of life and has won for his people an everlasting inheritance in the world-to-come. Already we are citizens of that kingdom and from the depths of our heart look forward to the day when the new heaven and new earth will be revealed. In so doing we acknowledge that our share in the world-to-come rests solely on the work of Christ.

In the present age, God has called his people to be citizens of heaven who live as pilgrims in this world. We do not take up the first Adam's task of earning, achieving, or in any way ushering in the world-to-come through our cultural labors, for Christ has already done this for us perfectly and sufficiently. Instead, we take up our cultural activities in grateful obedience to God and for his glory, recognizing that they are temporary and fleeting, always remembering that "the present form of this world is passing away" (1 Cor. 7:31). Though each of us at death "shall take nothing for his toil that he may carry away in his hand" (Eccles. 5:15), by faith we trust that God is pleased to use our cultural obedience to accomplish his inscrutable purposes in history and will acknowledge all of our good works on the day of Christ's return. Until then may we all take up our cultural activities with joyful and generous hearts, with charity to our enemies, and with the modesty and humility that befits the servants of Christ.

Scripture Index